Carmel Schulmeistrat

New Wine Press

New Wine Press
P.O. Box 17
Chichester PO20 6YB
England



ISBN 0 947852 85 9

Printed and bound in England
by Clays Ltd, St Ives plc

# Dedication

To Detlef, my husband and friend, and to my children, for your loyalty, commitment and love.

To Pastor Allen Richards for caring enough to "spend and be spent" never "shrinking back", and to Mary for believing in me!

Lastly, to my extended family in Christ at The New Life Centre, Bray, for your acceptance and prayerful support, which have proved so vital – this is not my story, but ours.

Victory is on our lips and in our lives!

# Contents

| | Page |
|---|---|
| Foreword | ix |
| Introduction | xi |
| Chapter One | 15 |
| Chapter Two | 31 |
| Chapter Three | 43 |
| Chapter Four | 49 |
| Chapter Five | 63 |
| Chapter Six | 79 |
| Chapter Seven | 85 |
| Chapter Eight | 92 |
| Chapter Nine | 100 |
| Chapter Ten | 109 |
| Chapter Eleven | 115 |
| Chapter Twelve | 121 |
| Conclusion | 127 |

# About the Author

Born in July 1951 in the heart of Dublin, Ireland, Elizabeth Carmel O'Connor had an unremarkable childhood but typical of many young Irish women of her generation.

Raised in a traditional Irish Catholic family, she was largely educated at a convent in one of the oldest parts of the inner city. Difficulties with the nuns there forced her to finish her studies in another school.

Leaving school at 18, she had a variety of jobs. Growing up and growing away from her family, she was desperate for answers to the questions that nagged her about life. She developed a growing interest in psychology and religion. And sought an escape in alcohol.

However, in 1972 her life suddenly changed direction when she really heard the gospel for the first time. She committed her life to Jesus Christ and was born again.

Married in 1972 to Detlef Schulmeistrat, Carmel is the mother of five children.

Since 1986, the Schulmeistrats have been members of The Apostolic Church in Ireland, having previously been employed as Houseparents at a Youth Conference Centre run by World Mission to Children in Austria.

Detlef is an elder in The Bray New Life Centre of The Apostolic Church and, from 1987 to 1989,

Carmel was leader of the Junior Church there. Since early 1990, she has led the Intercession Ministry of The Bray New Life Centre.

# Foreword

We are well informed through Scripture that for centuries men and women have walked around our world demonised. Only since the beginning of the ministries of our Lord has there been given to Man the answer to this terrible problem. The answer is Jesus Christ!

Many have thought and taught that by taking Jesus Christ as Saviour and Lord every past problem has been completely dealt with. How we wish this were true!

Undoubtedly, when we trust the Lord for our salvation he gives to us a complete and new creation birthed within us. It is perfect and entirely different to the old creature we used to be. Quickly this new creation emerges in our walk and in our talk.

Yes, the "butterfly" is emerging, but the old "chrysalis" is still hanging on. It is an undeniable fact that if in the past life we have opened the door to satanic powers through our old way of living, those powers are often still embedded in areas of our personality. Please note not always – but often!

Too often we deal with demonic powers like the children of Israel dealt with the old inhabitants of Canaan. They negotiated with them and suffered the consequences for the rest of their lives. God told them to cast them out. That is what we must do with demonic powers that may still be present resulting from our old way of life.

The contents of this book are a perfect example of the way that demonic forces tenaciously hold onto a life. It is also a perfect example that the power of the Name of Jesus can effectively deal with them.

Because I know Carmel, I can vouch for the truth and accuracy of this book. I commend it to you as a reader – praying that it will be a means of enlightenment and encouragement should you find yourself as a Christian in similar circumstances.

Samuel McKibben

Member of
The Apostolic Church Council
of Great Britain

# Introduction

I swung the car off the dual carriageway and headed into the Wicklow Hills. Even the thought of going home made me feel claustrophobic. I had to get out – get out of my head – get out into the good things of God's creation, the fields, the animals, the mountains. I rolled down the window, hoping the wind would blow away the events of the morning. The spiritual warfare I had experienced just a half hour before seemed so unreal and impossible out here in the "real" world, where the sun was beaming down and spring had most certainly sprung. I pushed in a music tape. "You are my everything, you are my all in all" began the first worship song. "I love this one," I remarked to myself, as my spirit began to soothe a little under the music's ministry. "You are my guiding light, the answer when I call". I winced as the reality of what I had been living with all these years was brought back by those words – the personal guiding spirit of destruction that had been cast out of my life this morning in the name of Jesus. How often had it in my ignorance been my guiding light? How often had it answered when I called for help? Just how much had I leaned and depended on its strength?

Suddenly I felt very alone and insecure, trying hard to ignore the fear that was beginning to gnaw at the pit of my stomach. "Lord God, surely there cannot be more?" I cried, knowing that I must not allow desperation or panic to take hold of me again – "I could not face it again, Lord".

Then I realised – no, the fear was not evidence of another demonic presence in my life – the fear was the reaction of my own soul, my spirit, my psyche, as it was exposed to life for the first time, alone and uncovered by this demon who had resided in the depths of my being for so long. So, this was freedom! The question now was – Could I live with it? Could I survive this period of transition from the security of dependence on the company and strength of demons to depending alone on the abiding Holy Spirit of God in my life?

I parked the car on the Sugarloaf overlooking the sea, trying to relax amid the memories of the morning. Some tourists strolled by, nodding politely. I was glad my sunglasses hid to some extent my bloodshot eyes and tearstained face. My body ached and my clothes were still soaked with perspiration. I wonder what they would think if they knew how I had spent the morning? I smiled wryly to myself. My consciousness was still back in that little counselling room, where our pastor, his wife and my husband had prayed with me and wrestled for hours with the ruling spirits of death, hell and destruction, until they were cast out of my life. In my heart I could still sense the horror, torment and suffering of that death spirit, could still see into that horrible pit of hell, worse than anything I had witnessed in man's inhumanity to man. What must the actual pit of hell be like? The beauty that surrounded me now made the horror even more repulsive. What would these people say? What would my neighbours say?

What would my family say if they knew where and how I had spent so many mornings like these in the last eighteen months? If they knew the number of evil spirits that had been cast out of my life in that time – if they knew the trauma and humiliation of a deliverance session, would they say, "This woman is a lunatic, a witch, a fanatic." What would they say if they knew I was an ordinary wife and mother, a born again Christian, a responsible citizen? What would the Christian world say? What would you say if you knew the story of "My Fight to Freedom"?

# Chapter One

Toronto, Canada, 1933. The young woman strained to hear what this old gypsy murmured to herself, as she gazed into her crystal ball, trying from the intensity in her spirit to project the future into this glass form. Desperately homesick, and still mourning the loss of her baby daughter, this young Irish emigrant had come in search of solace and hope, finding no conflict in her conscience between consulting this seer, and the fact that she herself was a devout Catholic. What was she saying? "A young man in army uniform? Many children? Ah, yes, in your old age, another daughter, but this one will break your heart!" A prophecy from the pit of hell, but my mother kept these things and meditated on them in her heart.

Perhaps then she should not have been surprised when I arrived in her 48th year in 1951, the last of a brood of thirteen. But surprised she was, and disappointed. Into a home where finances, accommodation, and not least emotions were already overstretched, I was born. It was the first year my mother had managed by shrewd budgeting to pare enough from the family income to pay for a holiday in Skerries. Now the money had to be spent on a pram for the new arrival! With my next-in-line brother now five years old, the home had again to be rearranged for another baby – the kitchen reorganised to house the cot that was to be home for me until I could walk. That was the way all her babies had been reared, my mother told me later. From this big cot they watched the proceedings of the household, the bottle propped up with a towel until they could hold it themselves.

In there, they were spoon fed and safely played out of the way of all the boisterous activity of the kitchen. This cot was large enough to accommodate a crawling baby, and eventually he or she would learn to walk, pulling himself up on the bars and swinging from one to the other like a little monkey. Very convenient in a busy home perhaps, but soul destroying for the child. It may have been from that little prison that I first developed the sense of being only an onlooker on life, a bystander – the sense that all of life went on without reference to, or consideration of me.

From my earliest days the clearest image of my mother is of her working at the kitchen sink, or cooker, with her back turned to me – always with her back to me. It seemed to epitomise our relationship all through my life. Long before I could understand or articulate it, perhaps even before I was born, I seemed to sense her emotional rejection of me. Of course I was fed, clothed and seen to in every physical way, but how I longed to feel loved and wanted; to be delighted in and accepted as a real part of this big busy family. Somehow, however, it was always too late, all the good times had been long before I arrived. "When all the kids were small," my mother would say "this happened and that happened", and the look on her face said that they were much less painful times than these present ones, with so many grown up problems to cope with, and me to put up with besides. I longed to make her happy to have me too, for there to be good times now, while I was small. Other children I know were in the habit of giving their parents gifts for birthdays and the like, so from time to time I tried this too. Unfortunately we were not a very demonstrative family, neither with our emotions or our gifts, and my offerings were soon discarded I noticed. There was no conscious intent to offend me of course, but the obvious lack of value to her of my actions and expressions, spoke loudly and clearly to my oversensitive spirit – "You do not matter". That seed of rejection sown so early in the soil of my heart, was fed and nurtured by these prevailing attitudes. It was eventually to grow and so choke my spirit that it became impossible for me to believe that anyone could ever love or value me. Worse still, it became impossible for me to accept or value myself. Having felt rejected by the most important person in my young life, I now rejected myself. The process of the disjointing of a personality had already begun.

Not surprisingly, with so many older sisters, I did not lack for surrogate mothers in my early years. Some of them were already in their late teens, already courting and dreaming their dreams, and they enjoyed wheeling me out in the pram on Sundays, with their boyfriends in tow, just for a little practice! Strangely though, none of their attention succeeded in forging that vital link between my parents and myself, and as they left the home, some to marry, others going abroad to work, the house became desperately lonely and empty. Christmas was wonderful of course, when our home became a meeting place for the whole clan again, brothers, sisters and faraway aunts and uncles gathered for the annual "hooley". Piano, pudding and party pieces, and not a little whiskey and guinness – the house was alive again for a day or two. But these days passed quickly, only to be replaced by oppressive emptiness again.

I was a quiet and studious child, so insecure that many minor childhood incidents became major traumas for me. Yet I never really talked to anyone about these things and they never seemed to ask. It was not until many years later that I learned from the Lord the full extent of the damage done to my personality through these situations.

One such incident was my first day at school. My older sister, Mena, was commissioned to deliver me safely to my classroom. Presumably my mother did not realise she was needed on what was to be a traumatic day. Suddenly I found myself in a strange area, since our school was miles from home. In this strange room, a strangely dressed person called a nun, was speaking to me in a strange language, namely Irish, and for reasons best known only to herself, refused to call me by my family name Eily, which I was accustomed to, but insisted on calling me by my middle name, Carmel. As the key turned in the door, locking me in with 50 other fretful children, panic took hold of me, and I suddenly found myself kicking and clawing at the locked door like a man buried alive, screaming for Mena to come and rescue me. Eventually the young nun had to give in and Mena was sent for, but unconsciously I had learned a valuable lesson that day. Out of my pure instinct for survival and self defence, I found that rebellion worked. Refusing to be comforted, I carried on until I got what I desperately wanted and needed, and somehow determined inside never to let anyone make me do what I did not like or want to do.

Now another seed had been sown, apparently to help me cope with the rejection and insecurity. It was to be many years before that seed of rebellion was to come to full bloom and try to destroy my life. But it was born out of an inability to cope with my situation. Many times later I was to lean on the strength of this rebellion, so often out of pure self defence. Several months later, disaster struck our home again in a way that was to have a life long effect on all of us probably, but certainly on me. It was the day before Christmas Eve – my mother was doing her last minute Christmas wash in the big tub and washboard, while I helped turn the handle of the old wringer. Mrs. Dale's Diary plays on the radio, while my "best" brother Joe, then fourteen, idled away the time swinging on the back of the kitchen chair. Suddenly he turned very pale, and cried out in pain, holding his chest. "Run and get Mrs. Clery!", my mother called to me in a tone that caused me to run as fast as my 5 year old legs could carry me. When I returned with our neighbour, Joe was covered up with a blanket on the armchair, his face now a peculiar purple colour. I was pushed aside as the two women carried him into my parents' bed in the parlour, but I did catch what was to be my last glimpse of him still alive. Drifting quietly on the periphery of the family as was my lifestyle, I picked up talk that day of doctors, relatives and heart trouble, but all I was told was not go to into that little parlour or disturb Joe. Then suddenly on Christmas Eve he had "gone to Heaven", they said. I did not know what that meant, all I knew was that everyone was very sad and quiet and neighbours and relatives came and gathered in the little parlour mumbling what must have been prayers. I had a peep, but Joe was not gone anywhere, he was just lying there very pale and still while everybody looked and mumbled, and his Meccano set for Christmas had already been opened; (had Santa come and not left me a present?). Again, my older sister was commissioned to amuse me in the kitchen while the removal service was going on. I do not know how she managed to pretend to be cheerful and play with me, but it did not seem to matter. Something serious was happening to my best brother and I desperately wanted to get into that room and find out what was going on. I was not allowed of course, the family wanted to protect me I suppose, and as always, since I was so quiet and introspective, I did not ask, and was told as little as possible. However, that "protection" imprisoned my grief all through my life. Sorrow and death became a part of my personality, a melancholy that even my friends could not understand in later years. I did not either. I still had the conscious memories of course, but the feeling had become disassociated with that incident, and yet every time I witnessed sadness or death, on the television or in life, I found myself grieving again as if I had lost my own flesh and blood.

Although there must have been many good days, my childhood seems to have been punctuated with traumatic situations which produced many fears within me. Fear of the dark, fear of water, fear of rejection, fear of authority. At one stage the insecurity got to such a state that at ten years of age, having emigrated to London, I tanked myself up every morning with Milk of Magnesia tablets to try to settle my stomach. Nobody guessed that anxiety and fear were the real problems.

As far as my school work was concerned, I need not have worried as I was intelligent enough and enjoyed learning. My teachers and I really only crossed swords on matters of discipline. Basically I was a little like a weed in a garden. Being the youngest of the family, and with the others so much older, there was little sibling rivalry to discipline me. Being quiet, I was not really cheeky or bold, I just became accustomed to doing my own thing, undisturbed. When the nuns found me being a nuisance in school, I developed the extraordinary ability to lie myself out of guilt so completely that I complained to the headmistress about the nuns' victimising and harassing me. I almost believed my own lies and adamantly refused to back down or apologise. It is amazing what pride will enable even a child to cover up. But these things have their long term effects, even if we think we get away with them.

At home, my parents seemed to be content to allow me to motor along as I pleased. Obviously I must have learned basic manners and social behaviour, but when it came to who was in charge of my life, even at a very early age, I knew that it was me. Firstly, because my parents did not want that responsibility. Although I was never abused by them in any way, their neglect of my needs emotionally and psychologically did immense damage, and left my life an open stomping ground for Satan and his demons. Knowing they had no real interest in me, and that I had no protection from them, I had to fight for survival with whatever means were available at the time.

And Satan saw to it that he provided a way and a means, but as the Word tells us that way leads to death and destruction. So, for every hurt that came my way, he provided the hatred and anger; for every inferiority, he provided the pride; for every abuse of my rights he provided self-will and rebellion that said "No one will ever do this to me again".

So I stumbled into my teenage years. With no input from my parents as to my future, I drifted into school, doing well considering I had so little motivation. It would have suited my mother to have me out earning some well needed money, for unfortunately she could not see beyond today, or see that education and encouragement would have made a much better future for all of us. I was blessed that one of my brothers could see ahead, and he did try to inspire and finance me to better things. However, the sense of my uselessness and inability overwhelmed what he tried to achieve. When I had trouble with one school, I asked to be changed to another, which I was allowed to do, provided I made all the telephone calls, contacts, etc. What I did when I left school was left entirely up to me. My brother wanted to send me to France to University since I was good at languages, but again, since all the enquiries and arrangements were left to myself, it fell flat on the ground, because I simply did not have the confidence or capacity to do all of this alone.

I was in every way unprepared for adolescence. Typically a time of self consciousness, I had plenty to be self conscious about as a fourteen year old. The skinny child was beginning to get fat, and definitely had the wrong shaped legs for the mini-skirted 60's. My hair was a frizzy mess, thanks to it having been permed for my Confirmation, and this was long before the Afro was cool! Thanks to a long neglected tricycle accident, my front teeth now had repulsive gaping holes, which my mother suggested might be filled with chewing gum when I broached the subject of doing something about them. Add to this an already warped self image and absolute ignorance of sex, and it is not hard to see that I had troublesome years ahead.

I ventured out into the world desperately longing for love and attention, to be held, to be touched, to be needed. A young girl in that condition does not have to look far for some boy or man – to even pretend for a little while. To my surprise, there seemed to be no shortage of boyfriends, but these relationships never lasted, and always seemed to end in further rejection. To bolster my confidence and ease the pain I began drinking more and more. When my parents began to raise their objections to my staying out late, the way I dressed, or anything else about me, I totally rebelled. I had long ago decided that they had no claims on me, that they had never been interested in me, and since they had shown me no love I would never allow them to stop me looking for it somewhere else.

They had never bothered about me while I was quietly "doing my own thing" and now that "my own thing" was causing some offence to them, "what would the neighbours think?" was something they would have to live with. As far as I was concerned, I had never asked them to have me in the first place, and from now on I was running my own life.

I have often wondered was Shakespeare quoting demons when he wrote "What a tangled web we weave, when first we practise to deceive", because having been deceived into choosing my own rebellious and wilful way, what a tangled mess my life soon became. As more and more of my time was spent drinking, drug-taking and generally being involved with situations and people that my family would have considered "undesirables", life became a complete fabrication of lies. Lies which they seemed to readily believe. With the lies of course, came enormous guilt and the pressure of having to cover my tracks all the time. As I got older and left school, I was becoming more dissatisfied and depressed, and even my friends were beginning to find it difficult to cope with my moodiness. In spite of the offer of good jobs (they were still available in the 1960's), I drifted from one job to another unable to put down roots in any one place.

I left home a number of times without trace, deciding to wipe my family out of my consciousness completely, as one of my greatest fears was of growing old and lonely, having to live out my life looking after my aging parents. My life seemed to become more and more one of denial of self. Rejection lured me into relationship after relationship, looking for someone to even temporarily ease the pain. I came out of all of them more hurt, more bitter, more angry than before. One part of my life was a litany of seedy pubs, seedy apartments and even seedier relationships. I could never share that part of me with my armchair philosopher friends, who despised drunks, druggies and anyone else who sought to escape reality in that form. Their time was spent escaping into their minds, splitting philosophical atoms, and catching political red herrings. Unfortunately, this lot seemed to need psychiatric help a lot sooner than those they despised. Then there were the nice neighbourhood groups, outdoor types, good living and religious, the kind my mother would have wanted me to settle down with. While they were fun for a time, my rebellious side found them decidedly boring, and I could not fit in with them either. There seemed to be nowhere I fitted into life and society.

Each group I ran with rejected the other types, and yet I was a part of them all. For fear of rejection, I was all things to all men in whichever peer group I found myself, and yet in being that

I was consistently denying myself. Small wonder that I was finding it more and more difficult to find any true identity.

As my school friends began to settle down with steady boyfriends and normal lives, I found myself more and more alone. So many times I found myself caught between the claustrophobic loneliness of my home, and spending yet another night with people and in places that could only add to my growing sense of self abhorrence. In my angriest and most determined moments I would swear I did not need anyone, and could be completely self-sufficient, but most often the need for even a pretence of friendship and love literally drove me out into the night. Of course pride and rebellion enabled me to keep face outwardly at least. But inside I was full of self-disgust and self-hate for even needing love. I knew I did not have the courage to take my own life outright, and yet I was in a downward spiral of self-destruction.

Somewhere in the midst of all this, my knight in shining armour galloped into my life on his white charger. As far as my family were concerned, he was anything but shining! As far as I was concerned, he was the biggest catch someone like me could ever hope to land – popular, handsome, charming, idealistic, and most importantly, he liked me! Or so he said. Then after some months of passionate teenage love, he was gone. What I understood to be a minor misunderstanding between us revealed the true depth or lack of, his love and concern for me, and I was shattered. Hell certainly has no fury like that of a woman scorned, and in my brokenhearted fury I would have gladly killed him, so scorching was my hatred for him now. In my sensible moments I considered he would not be worth doing time in prison for, but I did slay him with my words and attitudes whenever our paths crossed. Eventually of course, time did something with all these feelings. It certainly did not heal them, but it did bury them very deeply in my spirit, very much alive. It was to take some very deep and painful surgery at the hand of the Holy Spirit many years later to clear all these poisonous experiences out of my heart and life. Who but God would have undertaken such a project?

So where did God come into this picture? Well, like almost everyone else in this country, I had been raised on a staple diet of "First Fridays", "May Processions", "Guardian Angels" and "Plenary Indulgences". In my young teens I did join the Legion of Mary. Admittedly that was as much the attraction of the regular "socials", as anything else. These afforded me the opportunity of enjoying the dual luxury of cream buns for tea and dancing with boys!!! However, I did go through that period so many young girls experience of spending hours in the church, trying to find this God we had heard so much about through childhood. Our parish priest was so surprised to find me there alone one evening that he gave me his rosary beads, presumably to encourage me in my quest. However, as I read more and more about religion, philosophy, politics and psychology, in an effort to sort myself out, there were too many questions that remained unanswered. The fact that our religion made no real difference in our relationship as a family did not help us to love each other or to fulfil each others' needs. Then, as an idealistic young person, questions as to church wealth and world poverty could not be cast aside with a warning from a priest to avoid bad company and communist books. So, by sixteen years of age, I decided the Catholic Church was not for me and waited for the sky to fall. To my amazement, judgement did not fall from heaven, in fact life got neither better nor worse. Yet I could never deny that there was a God, although my image of Him was absolutely blurred and warped. I looked for him in Yoga, but again there was as much hypocrisy in the proponents of Yoga as I had seen in other religions. Diets, exercises and disciplines did not change their characters – not for the better at any rate. Transcendental meditation sounded so easy and so plausible, but I resented being inducted into a religious cult almost by deception. Not until we candidates arrived with our white handkerchiefs and flowers did we realise that we were to be dedicated to the guru Dev in exchange for our secret mantra. Even so, meditation, like Yoga, had one glaring drawback for someone like me. I was so depressed I could not concentrate on the magic word, and if I were together and disciplined enough to practice Yoga, I would not have needed it.

Then of course there was the grape cure to try – an endless diet of grapes – Norman Peale's Positive Thinking, hormone replacements, health food and vitamins for every ailment. Surely one of them would help to untangle the mess I was in, but unfortunately not – each one was eventually filed away under "F" for "Failure" – like myself. If there was a God who could help me, He would have to prove to be much bigger than any self-help technique, or religion. And that is where Jesus came in.

# Chapter Two

It was the Summer of 1972. Jesus was "making it big" on Broadway in the form of Jesus Christ Superstar. The Jesus people were sweeping across America and Arthur Blessitt was carrying his cross around the world. Jesus seemed to be on the streets of Dublin, too. The children of God were there, Ben Mosher and all the regular Abbey Street Corner Evangelists. It seems everyone was talking about Jesus in very familiar terms. I was familiar with his name alright, it punctuated my conversation regularly, but that was all. I had just celebrated my 21st birthday by having a final blow-up with my parents, leaving home and being invited never to come back. In spite of the efforts of other members of the family to create some understanding between us, things had gone too far. They had had enough of my lifestyle, my sullen moods and what I now see was my absolute selfishness and self-will. So here I found myself sharing a bedsit with other friends on the dole, opportunities of a College education and secure employment squandered, at war with the world, and mostly myself, simply living from day to day, and the future a nightmare.

I arrived home one evening to be told that my friends had invited a young Englishman to come and tell us more about Jesus. They had met him witnessing on the street and found him very sincere and convincing. I was surprised: we had talked a bit about all this "Jesus stuff", but I hardly thought they were that interested. I was even more surprised when the young man arrived – short hair, straight clothes, definitely not the type we would ordinarily associate with. But he did not seem to have any problem relating to us, and when he opened his mouth to speak about his friend "Jesus" in such loving and loyal terms, I knew this man knew Jesus in a way I never had. His Jesus was real, was alive, was a person, not some distant historical figure issuing laws and decrees from a faraway planet.

This Jesus he said, knew what it was like to be human, knew what it was to face the hassles of life, and yet had never run away. Never lied, never sinned – this Jesus knew what it was like to be alone and yet stood drawing His strength from the love of His Father. This Jesus could make me strong too. This Jesus had taken all my sins and my messed up past on himself when He died on Calvary, and he was now offering me a new beginning in life with him. A life of truth and honesty; of love, because he loved me enough to die for me, a clean and holy life, which my conscience longed for, and as if that was not enough, the promise of eternity spent in heaven with him. What? the matter of sin settled forever? No fear of hell? No years of torture in purgatory paying for every misdemeanour? A new life? It is not hard to guess that I jumped at the opportunity, and with the tiny amount of understanding I had, prayed with this young man, confessing my sins and asking Jesus to become my Lord and Saviour.

I did not have to be persuaded that I was a sinner, my conscience screamed that at me every "morning after the night before", although my pride always argued that I was not really like all the others who lived as I did. There were no thunderbolts, no flashes from heaven, no visions or supernatural phenomena when I prayed, but the first time in as long as I could remember there was a peace in my heart, a joy and such a relief to know the past was gone and forgiven. To my amazement as I awoke the next morning, it was still there. No shame, no guilt, no bad conscience, even though my circumstances had not yet changed the future looked hopeful, and all the foul language and blasphemy had been washed from my tongue. The holy one had come to reside in my heart – this was the reality of God I had looked for all my life.

The weeks and months that followed brought dramatic changes to my friends and myself, both to our lives and lifestyle. Although the young evangelist had returned the next day to England without putting us in touch with any church or fellowship, he told us to read our Bibles, believe, and obey what we read in them. Jesus is the only way, truth and life he showed us, and advised us to get rid of all our other religious and philosophy books.

At this stage, anything from Che Guevara to Sanskrit could be found on our shelves, so of course they were disposed of, just as the Ephesians did with their books and idols. Along with them went all our music of the so-called prophets of the 1960's and 1970's. When the Bible said

"Love not the world", we took it seriously, and made whatever changes were necessary, however radical. Any immoral relationships and situations we were in had to be changed no matter how painful the adjustments, and as for drinking or drugs, well, there was no need or time for that now. A small group of us lived in a community together, according to our limited understanding of The Acts of the Apostles which told us that the disciples were together and had everything in common. Now that we were working again and supporting ourselves, our leisure time was spent praying, reading the Word, Bible studies, Christian books, tapes. We cut our spiritual teeth on the best available teaching of those years. Our hunger and desire to know and serve God better was such that we had little interest in anything but Jesus. You could safely say my conversion was radical.

Obviously, the situation with my family had to be addressed. If I was now the new person I claimed to be, I knew I could not continue to avoid them. So by the grace of God I went back, apologised, and explained the situation and what had happened to me. I could not blame them for being somewhat sceptical after all they had seen of me in the past, and they probably had every right to be outright annoyed when I, in my innocence, explained that they also were sinners who needed to be born again. However, there was reconciliation between us although the relationship between my mother and I never really changed. Although I did endeavour to be the kind of daughter I should be, there seemed to be so much that could never be spoken about between us without a scene. However, although the family may not have been entirely happy with my new found "religion" no doubt they were relieved that my life was somewhat more settled now, if not exactly normal.

Our lives together in the community were not easy, but we certainly did learn quickly things that may have taken years in other circumstances. Learning to share, to consider one anothers' needs, to look after one anothers' interests did not come easily or naturally to young people accustomed to thinking only of themselves. On the other hand, the support of living in an environment completely devoted to Jesus and his word alone was invaluable. Yes, we often made mistakes in our ignorance and immaturity, but by the grace of God we grew. Having seen what the world had to offer, there was little temptation for me ever to go back to that way of life again. Yet of course the ways of the world run very deep in the flesh, as I soon found when the Holy Spirit began the painful process of bringing my life more and more into line with His Word. "It is the Spirit that gives life, the flesh profits nothing." With this scripture the Holy Spirit laid the axe to the root of any draw the world may have had from my earliest days as a Christian. Only the things of God, the things of the Kingdom, the things of the Spirit were profitable now for my life.

Some months after my salvation, the Lord brought a mature Christian our way who was able to teach us about the Baptism of the Holy Spirit and His supernatural gifts. Hungry for all that God had for us, we immediately said yes, and asked the Lord for this new measure of the Holy Spirit. Again, there were no flashes, no thunderbolts from the sky, but a quiet assurance that I had received what I had asked for. Finding myself praying in tongues, albeit falteringly at first, I knew that again something new and supernatural had occurred within me. This new dimension of the Holy Spirit in my life was to be a tremendous strengthening power in the years ahead, bringing with it a new depth of understanding and revelation of spiritual things.

In time, the Lord did lead us into contact with other Christians in Dublin. Older and more mature ones who helped us in our understanding of the Lord, and younger ones to whom we opened our home, which was then a rented house in Rathgar. From our understanding of the Bible, we perceived that there should be apostles and prophets even in this day, as in the Acts of the Apostles, but to our disappointment did not find them in any of the fellowships with whom we came into contact. So this became one of those issues that was put on "hold" as we got on as best we could with our Christian lives.

One year after I had become a Christian the Lord brought to our community a young man who was later to become my husband. A young German man, who had just come to know the Lord on his arrival in Ireland, and who was as enthusiastic and zealous for the Lord as my friends and I. Despite the enormous language barrier and cultural differences, we eventually married in 1976 after a somewhat stormy long distance relationship, and in the years that followed we had five lovely children. During the course of the following years, we had the opportunity and privilege of meeting and having fellowship with many other Christians throughout the country. The Lord used many of these brothers and sisters to add to our lives and help us grow. From some we learned the absolute need of leading a holy life, fully consecrated to God with others we experienced the healing power of Christian love and encouragement in the most practical ways possible. One term of eighteen months, we spent as "houseparents" to a Christian Youth Conference Centre, near Salzburg, Austria. This time certainly helped to broaden our view and heighten our level of acceptance of other Christians, as we met and worked with those of many differing nationalities, denominations and persuasions. Our labour for the Lord there was mostly of the uninspiring menial variety, but we did estabish many valued relationships which remained long after the memories of aching bodies had faded.

Through all of these experiences we came to appreciate the family of God and the oneness in Spirit of the body of Christ worldwide.

If I were writing a fairy tale or even a regular Christian testimony perhaps I might now close with the words "And they all lived happily ever after".

However, life is seldom like that, even for a hristian, especially for someone who had come into Christianity as scarred and confused as I had. Yes, knowing Jesus had brought only good into my life – he had given me direction, a goal, a purpose in life in serving him. But yet, there was still a huge void between what I read in the Word of that "Life so rich and abundant" and my day to day experience. That old sense of rejection haunted me wherever I went. No matter how involved in a situation or how committed to it, I never could feel quite part of things – I felt I was always on the outside, looking in. I could find no security even in my friendships from one day to the next. Today's time spent together might have gone fine, but tomorrow perhaps there would be something that would cause them to turn away from me. There was always a fear of being rejected again. Obviously this brought a great deal of unreality into relationships, because I was still trying to be all things to all men – what the Bible calls a "man pleaser" – in order to be accepted. Afraid to hold my own opinions, to make up my own mind, to be myself, always trying to show what I thought was my best side to people.

Even Detlef, my husband, could not persuade me of his love. No matter how often he told me, and in spite of the ways in which he did show his love and concern for me, something inside me refused to be convinced. The slightest criticism would have me sobbing in my pillow again saying that if he really loved me he would accept me the way I was. On those rare occasions when he did try to discuss issues that really did need changing, I was liable to withdraw for days at a time, so hurt and abandoned inside did I feel. I hated myself again for being such an emotional heap, for allowing myself to be vulnerable again, for even needing love. Needless to say, if I could not give or receive love from those whom I could see, how could I really believe in the love of a God whom I could not see? I knew the Scriptures very well that told me "God so loved the world", "God is love" and "He had proved His love in sending Jesus to die for us". But in my rejected mind His love meant that he tolerated me, put up with me, gave me a number with which I could enter Heaven. God would never really waste His attention on me – I was too inferior, too inadequate, too useless and unimportant. Not ever having been delighted in, or enjoyed and wanted for myself when I was young, it was now impossible to believe that anyone including God and myself could really like me now.

Not ever having learned as a Christian how to deal with these feelings, I unconsciously resorted to the old method – or I should more accurately say – I never changed from the old method, which was to defend myself by rebelling. So, depending on the prevailing mood of the day, criticism or crossing me in any way might cause a complete explosion of anger and rebellion, as my pride refused to accept that I was not always right in my actions and opinions. This treatment was generally reserved for my poor long-suffering husband, as I had sense enough to know that nobody else would accept this kind of behaviour from me. As much as I longed to serve God and be a good and submissive wife, so many aspects of my personality seemed to be out of control. How I longed for that meek and gentle spirit, which the scriptures said were so precious in the sight of the Lord. Knowing how often I was anything but meek and gentle persuaded me all the more that

God could never really love me. It is probably difficult to imagine that in the midst of all of this we actually had a good marriage, for there was a love and commitment to each other born of God that somehow withstood all of these storms. Detlef was always persuaded that some day things would be better, and that it would have all been well worth the trouble, in the end! A lesser man might well have found cause to abandon me to my mood swings and tantrums.

If things were difficult in the home, relationships with other Christians were a nightmare to contend with. As I have said, having such a fear of rejection by them, I could never let them know what I was really feeling inside. Yes, they could easily deal with my "rejection" days, and try to help me and cheer me up, encouraging me in God, but I knew I could never let them see the nasty side of me. So I tried always to be the good girl, although I am sure I did not fool all the people, all the time! Each situation I was in I found myself unconsciously and unwillingly "adopting" people, usually in leadership, as parent figures. All my desires for love, attention and appreciation seemed to fix themselves on these people, and although I was smart enough to know I had no right or claim to these people, I still could not control what I was feeling inside. This kind of situation inevitably led to my feeling rejected again, and brought with it such a jealousy of those who seemed to have and enjoy the relationships I so longed for. No matter how good the meetings or how blessed the fellowship, I could go home devastated if I had not had the attention of those I desired to possess. To my twisted reasoning, their love for others lessened my value to them, and of course, if I should ever express these things it would only serve to drive people further away from me. How often I wished I could take off to some desert island with just my family, and never have to relate to anyone else again. There seemed to be needs and longings and drives within me that could never be satisfied, and I could not understand how God had made me this way. Although the Bible said that Jesus had experienced humanity and knew what I was going through, I could not really accept that, since he had grown up in a family where he had been loved and wanted.

I was fairly sure that my problems related to my childhood and upbringing, and although I found no real way of undoing the harm, I strove desperately to avoid reproducing the same results in my own children. So many of my days were haunted with the threat of seeing my own children grow up just as messed up emotionally as myself.

Small wonder so much of my time was spent dealing with depression, sinus problems and recurring headaches, sometimes lasting days at a time.

So how did I relate all of this to my walk with God? Call myself a Christian and still feel and behave in such a way? Well, for fourteen years I led this dual existence. In as much as I could, I loved the Lord and longed to serve Him and to serve and love His people. So much of that fourteen years was spent heartbroken before Him – fasting, praying, struggling, and crying out to God to help me to become the woman I should be. I read and studied the Word, faithfully attended all the meetings I could, took time daily to spend with God, and did all the disciplines a Christian needs to grow, but with little lasting results. What made matters even worse was the fact that the very people who may have been able to help me and counsel me, were the ones I had the biggest problems with. I was well and truly trapped on this carousel of emotional hang-ups, and there seemed to be no way out, no one to turn to.

# Chapter Three

In 1986 the Lord directed us into the Apostolic Church in Dublin. There we heard the Word of God preached and prophesied as never before. Through the expounding and application of the revelation Word of God, we began to understand for the first time in our lives our true position in Christ, and our privileges as sons of God. Walking in faith and victory was not just for a chosen few, but was gloriously possible for every one of God's children. Going to Church on Sundays became so exciting that I could hardly sleep on Saturday nights, the Holy Spirit was moving in such a way. We as a family were really blessed by the balance of order and accountability in the Fellowship, on the one hand, and the liberty in the Spirit and practise of spiritual gifts on the other. We soon felt very much at home. The old questions we had long ago put on hold as to the existence of present day apostles and prophets and Church government, were finally answered to our satisfaction. Another subject we had put on hold some years before, was that of demonisation and deliverance from demons. Being very controversial subjects in the early 1980's, we had never quite come to any conclusions about it personally, but here we found in the Fellowship that God had begun to introduce this deliverance ministry, and people were being helped through it.

However, in spite of how good it was to have now found a spiritual home, it was not long before my old problems began to raise their ugly heads again. I awoke one morning and found all the excitement was gone. My faith was gone. God was gone – inside I was full of fear and depression. Although the members of the Fellowship had welcomed and accepted us, I was finding it very difficult to get over the sense of insignificance I felt, and soon I was struggling with rejection and jealousy all over again. However, I praise the Lord that this time there was help available in the form of our pastor, Allen Richards, and his wife Mary. Detlef saw to it that I sought their help, literally dragging me into the pastor's office the first time. Imagine my embarrassment when Detlef announced to the pastor, "Carmel is having a problem with you, she seems to think of you as some kind of father-figure, and is feeling very neglected". To my surprise, Pastor was not the least perturbed by such a revelation, and tried to help and counsel me all he could. It was to be a long time before I could talk to Pastor and Mary about all the horrible things going on inside me, but at least I could begin to trust them and open up sufficiently to get some very positive and relevant direction and counselling into my life. Under the ministry of God's Word my faith did begin to grow now in a new way. We were taught just how alive and powerful was every word that proceeded from the mouth of God, that the seed of the word planted in our lives was powerful enough to grow all by itself and change us into the image of God. We were called out of the Christian Struggler's

Club to reign in this life as more than conquerors through him who loved us. God was presented to us as our loving heavenly Father, in whom all our needs could be met and in whom we could find all our emotional security and self worth. I wanted to believe and live in the reality of these things with all my heart, but try as I may, something deep down inside of me refused to be convinced.

By 1988 a new Fellowship had been established in Bray, as many people from the North Wicklow area had been travelling to the Fellowship in Dublin now for some time. It was good to be part of what God was doing in His Church. My husband Detlef was a member of the leadership team, later to become an Elder in the Fellowship, and I was given the task of setting up and leading the Sunday School. I had always enjoyed working with children and wanted them to grow up with the best they could receive from God. I longed to have a really effective, spiritual ministry to these children, and during the Summer months set myself aside to fast and pray, to seek God for a new anointing on my work among them.

By this time I had come to know and love our pastor and his wife Mary, and had spent many hours sharing and receiving counselling from them. That so many of my problems were rooted in the distant past was obvious. Yet, even just talking about them did not seem to bring lasting relief or healing. They would constantly reassure me that the blood of Jesus was sufficient to cover the past, and that God could, and would, restore the years the locusts had eaten. I was directed back into the Word of God to find God's answers for all my problems and to renew my mind. Yet although I worked hard to apply God's promises to my life, I often would see improvements for only a few days. I would soon find myself embroiled again in the struggle with rejection and depression, or with that rebellious streak that said "nobody will tell me what to do". From time to time I would say to them – "do you think I need deliverance?" and they would reply "Well, we will see in time, but first you have got to do all you can to walk in victory on the basis of God's word."

As we moved into autumn, I sought to put new ideas into practice, to seek new approaches with the children – yet instead of feeling more fulfilled, I actually found myself growing increasingly agitated. I was still unconsciously at that stage of finding my identity and importance in what I was doing for God, rather than simply what I was. When my insatiable appetite for attention was not satisfied with constant praise and appreciation, I became more and more frustrated and angry; angry at the leadership for not congratulating me on the wonderful work I thought I was doing; angry at the parents who were not as eternally grateful to me as I thought they should be; angry with God for giving me a behind-the-scenes job, while others were receiving the spiritual gifts and ministries I thought I deserved. In short, just absolutely, utterly, selfishly, angry.

Obviously I was doing my best to keep these feelings well covered up and battened down, at times having to withdraw from people completely, for fear of what I might do or say that would cause irreparable damage to relationships. Many an hour I spent on my knees before God, crying out to Him to take these feelings away. The hardness of my own heart was beginning to frighten even myself – how could I ever love and encourage God's people feeling this way?

# Chapter Four

My heart leaped with fright as the young girl's scream broke through the worship music. "Not again", I thought to myself. It was not very long since we last had heard a demon cry out through somebody else in one of our meetings, and witnessed its public deliverance. Yes, I knew it was all right and true, yet I somehow found it all a little discomfiting. I could accept that some of the new converts in the Fellowship would need deliverance from demonic strongholds, as they came into the Kingdom from such messed up backgrounds, but did we have to have our meetings interrupted like this all the time? Besides, to my amazement, this girl had been a Christian since she was eleven years old, and although her family were not Christians, she had never left the "straight and narrow". Certainly not to the extent that I had as a teenager. If she had a demonic problem, what were the implications for me? I put the thought aside and prayed vehemently in tongues, in as much of an effort to hold myself together as to support the ministry being conducted. When things had quietened down a little, the convenor of the meeting, the pastor, reassured yet challenged us. He said "if the Holy Spirit is working in the meeting in a particular way, convicting, healing or delivering, and we find ourselves disapproving of His work, then we must ask ourselves – are we in the Spirit at that moment? Surely the Holy Spirit does not contradict Himself? – there ought to be an Amen in our spirit to His working among us." I was now feeling decidedly uncomfortable. As was our practice from time to time, we then spent some moments simply greeting one another, reassuring each other of our love and commitment to one another come what may. As I met Pastor Richards he said to me, "I am praying for you Carmel, God will do it". Now what will I do with that statement I wondered? "God will do it" – God will do what? When your pastor is someone not given to wasting words, you do go home wondering what on earth was he talking about. Did he mean that which I had been seeking the Lord for in connection with the childrens' ministry? Did he mean God's general plan and purpose for our lives?

I tossed and turned all night – something told me something serious was afoot. On awakening next morning I immediately asked Detlef – "Have you been talking to Pastor about me?" "What do you mean?" he asked. I explained what had happened the night before – "do you know what he meant by saying 'God will do it'? Does he mean what I have been praying about, or something else?" I faltered, knowing by his expression that the something else was something I did not want to hear. "Well," Detlef said gently " – your behaviour has been so irrational lately, that I asked Pastor if he thought you might need deliverance." Explosion!! For an hour I ranted and raved at how he had no right to go talking to other people about me, how I would never trust him or

Pastor again, that he was just as bad and had as many problems as I had, and so on, and so on. (It really did prove how unprepared for the truth I had been in the past when I had actually asked if I needed ministry). Detlef wisely said nothing. However, by the time I had sent the children off to school, all I could do was throw myself on my knees before the Lord and acknowledge yes, it was probably true. Only that week had I not read several times in the Psalms that the rebellious live in a parched land – that before God rebellion is like the sin of witchcraft? That gentle Holy Spirit had been trying to prepare me, but I had not recognised His voice. I wept and wept. I had so often cried and repented of my sins, I thought, but now the enormity of my sinfulness before God seemed to consume me in a new way, and all I could say was "Woe is me for I am undone". Imagine me before God as guilty as a witch.

I could hardly speak for two days so shocked and sickened with myself did I feel. Me, with a demon working in my life? If I had had any doubts, they were soon dispersed that Sunday morning at our meeting. Through all the years of ups and downs, I had still always been able to take part in worshipping God and learning from His word, but today was different. All through the meeting something horrible and almost nauseating as going on inside me as the presence of God was manifested among us. I thought at best I would pass out, at worst I might freak out publicly and make a show of myself. I tried to catch my husband's eye to do something to help me, as panic was rising inside. I got through those few hours only by refusing to concentrate on the things of God, and watching the children playing outside. By the end, I was so visibly shaken and disturbed that a number of people came and said "Gosh, are you getting the 'flu or what? You look absolutely shattered." If only it had just been the 'flu. Before we left, Detlef and I approached the pastor, but at that stage hardly needed to explain anything, as my face told the whole story. Yes, they had known for some time, but had to wait for God's time, when He would reveal my need to my own heart. Only then would I be ready to receive deliverance. They were extremely sensitive and kind, assuring me that we are all sinners, saved only by God's grace, but I felt like the vilest thing that ever walked the face of the earth. Sixteen years as a Christian, and still in this condition – I was thoroughly ashamed of myself.

Arrangements were made for me to come for prayer on Tuesday. "Go home fast and pray and get into the word in preparation," I was told, "and just one thing, when you come, do not try to dress all the problems up nicely. If you are ever to get free you will have to let it all out exactly as it is." So I did as I was told, and somehow, held out until Tuesday morning. Eventually it was time to go and we set off, with me in a very nervous and agitated condition. My greatest fear was that with all my hang ups and inhibitions, I would not be able to let anything out. I was soon to find however, that I need not have worried.

We sat in the living room waiting for Mary to join us. Outside in the kitchen I could hear the ladies chatting. "How can they talk about such trivialities when my life is falling apart here?" I thought. Pastor was nonchalantly humming a chorus to himself, trying to be lighthearted and congenial. I wanted to scream at him to be quiet. Eventually Pastor, Mary, my husband and myself were in and settled. Pastor began by reminding me "Now Carmel, some of these problems as we have explained to you before may simply be areas of your flesh life you are going to have to work on".

I could feel myself relaxing – off the hook – "but," Pastor continued, "we are just going to pray now and ask the Lord for His direction." Thirty seconds or so into the prayer, the spirit of anger was beyond my control, and before I really knew what was happening, it had been cast out of my life in the name of Jesus, screaming like an angry pig. I fell into Mary's lap absolutely mortified and yet relieved; something real had definitely happened. Since we knew rebellion was certainly a problem I had, they began to address this spirit. It manifested by stubbornly refusing to leave. As I sat there, the Holy Spirit began to bring before me the many incidents from even my childhood that had given this enemy a foothold in my life. The first day at school, the later defiance of my teachers, my attitudes to my parents in my teens. These had to be confessed and renounced by me, before this spirit's hold on my life could be broken. But broken it was, and it too had to bow the knee and leave in the mighty Name of Jesus. Hot on his heels was cast out the spirit of rejection, who left crying – "Nobody loves me." I was exhausted, but strangely calm. We looked at the clock – we had been there for less than two hours. Two hours, after thirty-seven years of turmoil, and these things were gone from my life! It was almost unbelievable. I felt as if I had had a limb amputated, so much of that inner strength was now gone. Detlef took me home to rest, leading me like a little lamb. I now was so weak, so vulnerable, and in a sense, so empty inside.

The next days were very strange, as I sought to come to terms with the traumatic experience of deliverance. My mind turned over and over all that had happened, all that was said. Was that really me in that room? How could I live with myself knowing that evil spirits had spoken and acted in such a way through me? Had I lived my whole Christian life actually in rebellion against God? Had all the years been wasted? The pastoral aftercare now proved so essential. So many questions needed to be answered and I needed so much reassurance and love. With the spirits which had influenced so much of my thinking now gone, my mind seemed blank for some time, and it was impossible to make decisions. All I could safely do was to read scriptures and even they had to be chosen by my "Everyday with Jesus". I was so thankful to have Detlef, so understanding and supportive, helping me through those difficult days. However, I soon began to feel the benefit of what God had graciously done for me. Now that the "fight" was gone out of me, our home life immediately became peaceful and agreeable. So it had not just been my Celtic temperament after all! I began for the first time to really enjoy my husband's love and the love of my children. I was no longer "locked outside" of my church family and friends – for the first time I began to feel a part of things. It was as radical as getting saved all over again, and my husband was delighted with his "new wife". I hoped and prayed that would be the end of deliverance for me – little did I know I had just taken the first step on what was to be a long road to freedom.

I awoke again in a lather of perspiration. It was that dream again. I had dreams like it often in the past, but this was the fourth time this week. What was going on? Nothing happened in these dreams to frighten me, and yet they were strangely disturbing. There was usually a different man, an ordinary setting, nothing immoral said or done, and yet there were unspoken overtones that I found strangely disturbing. Why should I dream about other men at all? My marriage was good and fulfilling, in spite of our difficulties. I had never been interested in any other man in that way since I had met my husband. In the past I thought such dreams were perhaps the enemy trying to feed temptation into my mind, but now it was recurring so often and so clearly, that I was beginning to grow suspicious. It was two weeks since my deliverance and although I recalled the experience still with a sense of trauma and pain, there was something else of which I was very suspicious. The nature of spiritual warfare in deliverance ministry had involved some physical contact with the minister, in the laying on of hands, and so on. To my horror, as I recalled the incident, I realised there was a part of me that actually enjoyed that contact in a wrong way. Was this connected with the dreams? Was there something going on subconsciously within me which I had never been aware of? How was I going to deal with this? If there was a demon at work however hidden, how could I ever tell anyone, in order to get delivered? Yet, how could I ignore it? After all, the Lord had been impressing upon me so much in the last days that scripture verse "*If I regard iniquity in my heart, the Lord will not hear me*". If I knew there was a problem, and chose because of embarrassment to simply go on living with it, I need not waste my time praying to God about anything else – He simply would not be listening. Here, I was caught in the old trap again!

As I waited on God through the week, I realised that it was going to be impossible to ignore what was going on. Situations from those teen years and relationships long confessed and repented of, were brought back before my minds' eye by the Holy Spirit. But this time, for the first time, I was seeing them as God saw them. Yes, I had seen them as immoral and damaging to all concerned. Yes, I had changed my lifestyle, but now I saw with revulsion the filthiness of my sin in this area: I was "as a worm in my own sight" as I acknowledged "against thee, and thee only have I sinned".

I decided to "test my case" with an old friend who had been involved extensively in counselling. After all, there was less risk in sharing with her, than at that point going to Mary. Oh, I knew Mary would help me alright, but my fear was that she would never trust me with her husband again. Well, would you? Tearfully, I poured out the whole sorry mess to my friend. Could it be demonic? Would I have to tell pastor, and could I ever be free?

To my consternation, but relief, the answer was "yes" to all three questions. It was quite possibly a demonic problem, and if so, I certainly could get free, but I would have to share the situation with the deliverance minister. What a challenge now to my motives. Lord, I prayed, how can I tell them, and how can I ever look them in the eye again? The Lord's reply was quite clear – "Alright, suppose they never will trust you again, are you still prepared to risk losing this relationship for the sake of having the future right with Me?"

Painfully embarrassed I spoke to Mary, who did not seem at all put out. I did not realise of course, that they had come across such problems often in their ministry. I thought I was the only one. Again a time was set for me to be prayed with, and off I set again with much fear and trepidation. To my horror, when I entered the room, there were several other people present chatting away calmly. I waited for them to be asked to leave, but there was no sign of that happening. As pastor began to talk with me and ask me questions I was getting more and more panic stricken. Surely he did not expect me to talk about such things in front of other people – it was hard enough as it was. "They cannot just land this on me without asking me or preparing me in some way," I thought. "They have no right to violate my rights like this."; I could sense the old defence mechanisms springing into action, but I knew if I allowed that attitude to take over, I might as well go home. Only with a humble and contrite heart could I get deliverance. Somehow I kept myself under control, and the prayer proceeded. But worse was to come. Having dealt with some fears, they then began to address the spirit of lust. I wanted to scream – "now hold on a minute, I know I may have some problems, but lust! that just could not be. I am just not that kind of person. I am a nice girl, ask my husband". For all my promiscuity, I had never seen myself behaving in the fashion that the term "lust" suggested.

Since I was obviously resisting the ministry, they stopped to investigate what was going on with me. I just could not have a spirit like that I insisted. I am not like that. Eventually, they calmed me down, explaining what a spirit of lust is and what it does. It is Satan's perverted form of love. When a soul like mine has been starved of real love, it can turn to the sensual world for satisfaction. Persisting in that kind of behaviour can cause the person to become demonised in that area, and they find themselves driven from situation to situation, deeper and deeper in sin, all the while the real need for love never being met. Although I was now a Christian for a long time, and had turned away from that way of life, that spirit had gone "into hiding" so to speak, and had been trying to influence my behaviour in ways that I might never have detected. However, the enemy had overstepped himself with the dreams in the last week and had unwittingly revealed his presence. The Lord had uncovered him and he was now about to be cast out of my life. Glory to God.

But how was my husband coping with all this knowledge about his wife? How would this affect our marriage? Would he be able to accept me? I almost felt as if I had been unconsciously unfaithful to him, although I had never wittingly given myself to such a thing. His response again humbled and amazed me – "what I do know already is forgiven, and what I do not know does not matter anyway – I love you." By the grace of God, I could now face the truth and having renounced the spirit it soon had to leave. Once again we went home rejoicing in the power and goodness of God. The dreams stopped immediately. To my surprise I began to notice a change in the way I related to both men and women. There had been a time when I would have said I quite innocently preferred male company to female company, finding them more interesting and stimulating in conversation. Now I found myself not nearly as interested at all in men, and began to really enjoy and appreciate the friendship of other women. What an undercover worker this spirit of lust had been. It had had me fooled into thinking this was an intellectual and spiritual rapport I had with men. It had disguised its sexual nature knowing that as a Christian I would never have willingly gone along with it. But the Spirit of God, who knows all things, had not been fooled, and had now set me free. Praise His name.

I was now looking forward to my first Christmas as a free woman. Well, freer at least. To my abject disappointment, I found my joy was very short lived. The effects and improvements from my deliverance remained, but yet I was still finding myself upset by so many situations and people that at times I wondered if all the old problems or demons had come back. I longed for that peace and security in God that nothing or nobody could take away, but it was still a long way off. I found myself in the depths of depression again, fighting hard to stay in faith and victory, and yet such were the extremes of emotions and reaction that I felt, I soon suspected the worst. Perhaps there were more "squatters" needing to be evicted from my life. How could I go through Christmas with the family in such turmoil?

However I felt the work of rebuilding the old broken down walls still had to continue. Certainly the things I had been delivered from now no longer had a hold on me, and in each situation I now had a choice to walk God's way, whereas in the past there had been no real choice in the demonised areas. My reactions "reacted" before I had had time to even think about situations. Many hours of many days and nights were spent in intense spiritual warfare as the old problems sought a way back in, and as new ones were being stirred up by the Holy Spirit. Only in the Word of God could I find and keep my sanity. Scriptures had to be written down and posted at eye level in every room of our home, where they could be constantly ministered into my mind and spirit. Some days the only way the oppression could be lifted was by actually walking around the house reading and declaring the scriptures to myself and the demons, at the top of my voice.

I had also come to realise the fact that I could not afford to allow any demons or inner conflict to keep me from the discipline of my Christian life, no matter how hard or uncomfortable that might be. Each time I received deliverance, it was so necessary to come back to God and give thanks to Him "in the midst of the congregation". Even if I was in turmoil when I came to a meeting, I could still determine with my will, to praise God, to pray publicly even if all I could do was to declare that Jesus is my Lord. Each declaration, each stand that was taken consolidated the ground taken back from the demons, and let any remaining ones know that their days were numbered. In this way, by the grace of God, the will and determination to get free was being strengthened all the time. As long as we are passive, demons will never move.

As a result of the rejection and desperately low self-esteem I had had, my thoughts and words had been consistently negative. Sitting under the ministry of the positive faith-filled Word of God which was being preached within our Fellowship, eventually I began to grasp the fact that the "joy of the Lord" was not just a good feeling I should desire for myself, but a fruit of the Spirit which I had a responsibility to develop in my life. This fruit of joy could not grow from the weedbed of negative doubts and fears which was my thought life, and I now understood how very self-destructive such thought patterns were. God knows how He created us to function properly, and the scriptures that tell us to forget the past and think only on good things are not optional extras to help us to feel better; they are absolute necessities for a healthy mind and life. It was clear that the painful memories of the past were going to have to be completely dug out and the all-pervading melancholy dealt with if I was ever going to enjoy the experience of a renewed mind and life.

# Chapter Five

Over the Christmas holidays I pondered much on what I was feeling, asking God to help me understand. Although delighted to have been set free from that spirit of lust, my pride had really taken a beating. I felt scorched inside every time I recalled what had happened, and the fact that others knew such things about me. Whatever false self-image my pride had built for myself was now badly tarnished, and it was difficult to live with myself. Obviously this also made me very difficult to live with, and I found myself again withdrawing from my friends. At least my work in the Sunday School gave me a good excuse for remaining in the background in our Fellowship and I was thankful that I could legitimately "disappear" behind the busyness of organising classes, lessons and teachers.

Even worse than my hurt pride was the distressing fact that I still felt so threatened and jealous of others. My jealousy was not of possessions, but rather of relationships, I realised. In my longing to be special to those who were special to me, I could not cope with anyone taking my place or getting in my way. As for sharing my friends with others, that brought all the old feelings of rejection again. As I searched out the Scriptures about this, the Lord began to show me the seriousness of this negative emotion. I wrote in my diary these notes:-

"Jealousy and envy are very destructive forces. They drove Jesus to his death (the Bible says the Pharisees were jealous of him). Envy caused Joseph's brothers to sell him and want to kill him. Jealousy begrudges others doing better than one's self. It can cope with those weaker, but only as a sense of comforting superiority. Jealousy cannot rejoice with those who rejoice because it resents their going on in God and is threatened by this. It works against people and also against God's work in their lives. It is as destructive as murder and hate and would lead to these if allowed. Jealousy cannot approve what the Spirit of God is doing in someone else. *It is impossible to serve others with this present* – as one will only minister to others to bring them up to a 'handleable' level – not to get the best for them, as this could threaten one's own position."

In the course of my working on this emotional problem, the Holy Spirit brought back to my mind an incident which had happened when I was perhaps eight years old, and this appeared to have been the first opening through which the spirit of jealousy had first obtained a foothold. I had never known my mother to be anything other than she was with me, which was cold and distant. On this occasion, a little girl about my age, and also called Carmel, was brought to stay in our home for a few days. She was a relative by marriage, and her mother was long dead. At this stage her father was also at the point of death and it was thought best for us to take care of her for a while. Due to the lack of space in our little home, my mother, Carmel and myself, slept together in my parents' bed, with the little stranger cuddled up between my mother and I, a fact which put my nose out of joint to begin with. As I lay there in the darkness almost asleep, I overheard my mother break the news to the little one that her Dad had died just that night. I was very sad for her, but what caused me even more bewilderment was the way my mother spoke and comforted the child, in loving and tender tones such as I had never heard or received. I had never really known what I was missing until I witnessed it; never known she was capable of such affection or how much I longed for it. Now here it was for the first time, but it was being poured out on somebody else. In spite of feeling sorry for the little girl, my childish heart was filled with jealousy of the fact that she was receiving the love that was rightfully mine. The door was opened that night in my heart to the spirit of jealousy that was to torment me all my life, seeking to ruin all my friendships and relationships. Whoever I fixed my affection upon, from them I sought constant assurance that I was the most important person in their lives. Of course, this totally unbalanced demand was rarely spoken out, but rather read or misread from their attitudes to me and their relationships with others. This "green-eyed monster" within ensured that I saw and heard every little situation as a threat to myself, and every new gift or ministry released in the Fellowship simply meant that God Himself had overlooked me again. Jealousy was to prove to be one of the last and most heart-breaking spirits to be cast out of my life, as I judged my progress in God by the measure of threat I felt from people and situations.

With two months of rebuilding and preparation now complete, Pastor Richards felt it was the right time in God to deal with what the Lord had shown me was influencing my life. This would be the third deliverance session and the eternal question seemed to be – would it be the last? As I suspected, a spirit of pride was indeed present, and he was soon cast down from his lofty stronghold through the authoritative prayer in the Name of Jesus. The session continued with the ministers looking to the Lord for discernment and guidance. A spirit was definitely reacting to the challenge of the name of Jesus, but insisted it would not leave or did not have to, because I was unwilling to let it go. As we paused to talk this through, I was quite amazed and confused. This was a spirit of self-will and I had no idea of what it was or how it had become such a strong part of my personality. It was apparent that somewhere in the past I had determined that I would do only what I wanted to do, and in my way and time, and that no one was going to tell me otherwise. Somewhat different from rebellion which reacted against authority, self-will stubbornly insisted on having its own way. This stubbornness had become a demonic stronghold which constantly worked against my true desire to work with others, to be flexible and to flow in real unity even with my own husband. Something inside always demanded that things must go my way, and I suffered terrible frustration when this did not happen. Of course,

I thought it was me seeking my own way, but in fact it was really a demon seeking its own way which would surely be a way of destruction. Yet this demonic entity had become so much a part of my personality, that it was now extremely difficult to understand how to renounce and repent of it. To me it seemed that I would be renouncing my own rights as a human being, my own right to will and to choose. Would I be leaving myself vulnerable to somebody else taking over my life? Gradually the realisation dawned that whereas I thought for years that I was defending and protecting my rights, I had in fact been defending and protecting demons, and the endless arguments and bad humours with my husband had been part of the enemy's plot to destroy our relationship. It was a huge step of faith to launch out into the unknown and declare my willingness to now submit my will completely to a God whom I did not yet really know.

However, by His grace I was enabled to do what was necessary and was soon delivered of this spirit. It was only in later conversations with Detlef and Pastor Richards that I discoverd to what extent I had carried the stamp "handle with care". I had always seen myself as easy going and approachable, and so I probably was, when it suited me to be. They however had seen the other side, stiff-necked and intransigent at times, and had learned to be cautious in approaching me with suggestions or directions. One never really knew what reaction would be forthcoming in such situations.

In every area of counselling and deliverance,

forgiveness plays a major role, as the Word tells us that unless we forgive others, God cannot forgive us. Through the several deliverance sessions I had experienced, I was beginning to understand the importance of deep repentance from my sins, and of true forgiveness for the sins of others. Repenting of my own sins was not really so hard, especially when God had revealed the awfulness of it, to my own heart. Forgiving others, however, did not come so easily. Both the hurts of the distant past and the minor everyday offences I found so difficult to put aside. In 1 Corinthians 13:5 it says "*Love does not even notice when it is offended*" (Living Bible). I longed for that to be my experience. I said I forgave; I really thought I forgave. Yet, every incident, every person, every occasion that had really hurt me in the past was as alive in my memory years later, as the day they had happened. Every deed done, every word spoken, all the emotions felt were still as sharp and clear as ever. As we sat in that little room the pastor told me, "You will have to forgive these people; speak out your forgiveness, if you are ever to get free". It was almost impossible. Unforgiveness had become such a stronghold in my life through the years, that a spirit now ruled there that said "No, I will never forgive them; I hate them, why should I let them off the hook?"

"Lord," I prayed, "I want to forgive. Please help me". But no, that prayer just was not sufficient, I was counselled. I would have to decide as a matter of my will, to forgive and speak out my forgiveness, before this stronghold could be broken. How could I do such a thing? To simply forget the hurt and disappointment these people had brought into my life meant that they were getting off "scot-free" and unpunished for what they had done. I had been rejected and denied real love all along, and now if I let the bitterness go, I would be left with nothing. As the realisation grew of how the enemy had been the cause of it all, right from the beginning, and that even the unsavoury pleasure I now had in despising others was itself demonic, I grew very angry with these demons and cut them off in the Name of Jesus.

Amid the conflict of the flesh crying out for justice, and the demand of the Word of God to forgive, it was still possible to determine with my will to do the right thing, opening the way for deliverance from this unforgiving spirit. We had come to the end of another gruelling deliverance session, made more difficult because these were major strongholds in my life, and did not easily give up ground, and also because I was still only learning how to cooperate with the ministry and to conduct the internal warfare necessary for a speedy deliverance. Praise God, however, it had been very successful and I again began to see major changes in my life. Those painful memories began to fade now, and I could look at the people involved at least with a measure of compassion because they too had their own problems which had caused them to be as they were. I had always tried to understand and acknowledge this in the past, but that acknowledgment had never succeeded in easing my own pain. Only with deliverance came healing at last.

As often happened, after deliverance came revelation from the Holy Spirit as to how and why these demons had influenced my life. In the days following this deliverance, I wrote the following notes in my diary:-

"Much of the rebellion of the past, the self-will and independence have been my reaction to the sense of being a 'nobody'. It seemed that as a child, everything was done over my head and without my cooperation, thus breeding in me a determination for 'self-determination'. I can see that I have been defending and trying to establish myself just to survive, in situations where people may not have meant to harm me, but where I felt my will was being violated. I am beginning to see that God is not like that. He is a gentleman, He does not lord it over us. I can let that 'self' go in the knowledge that I can trust Him never to go over my will, never to violate my right to choose, but that He works in me to will and to do His good pleasure. He is love and loving. He will prepare me for His will. We will reason things out together, and because I will grow to trust and love Him, because He loves me, I will want to do His will. I will want to be the person He wants me to be and do what pleases Him, because I will love Him. Although jealousy did not appear to go, the Holy Spirit has been showing me why I have felt constantly threatened by people. I have been like a bear with a sore paw, a wounded animal, defend-

> ing myself and my corner from anyone or anything that came remotely within shooting distance of me or mine. My hurt has made me supersensitive and in most situations people (especially the Christians) have never meant to slight or hurt me. I have been defending myself often when I have not needed to. I have to allow God to be my defender now, to take refuge in Him alone, and also begin to trust people, knowing that not everyone intends to offend, slight or hurt me. 1 Corinthians 13 says, '*Love always protects*'. The God of love will always protect me, not attack me, and His love in His people will be the same".

With these spirits of pride, self-will and unforgiveness now gone, I began to feel amazingly alive. I had never realised how much emotional energy had been taken up with carrying the past and running the present. My physical appearance was beginning to change, and many people remarked on how bright and relaxed I was looking these days. Obviously, apart from those involved in my counselling and deliverance, no one would have known or guessed all that was going on inside. After all I was a good Christian, and good Christians are not supposed to feel these things, and so all of these harmful and sinful emotions had to remain hidden away behind my mask. I now found that all the energy and drive that had gone into coping with life had to be redirected and I threw myself initially into many creative activities for which I had never had time before. Falling in line with my husband's plans and suggestions now came much more easily. To his delight, I was now able to enjoy family activities like hill walking, which I would have only grudgingly joined in with before.

It was at this point that Pastor Richards, from his study of other material on demonisation, began to observe the "schizophrenic" pattern emerging in my deliverance. Put briefly, schizophrenia whether acute or mild, means that there is present in a person a split personality or more than one personality. In a matter of moments, the person can switch from one to the other, causing great confusion to those around them. Arising out of the root of rejection, a completely self-denigrating personality is built up, with strongholds of self-rejection, inferiority, insecurity, lust, guilt, fears, and so on. In an effort to cope with this internal torment, another compensating personality is built up full of rebellion and pride and hitting back at the world that has caused the damage and pain, supposedly defending itself from it. Somewhere buried under these extreme personality traits is the real personality, which has never been allowed to develop and grow into maturity. Such a person is constantly at sea as regards his true identity, and is at least an emotional cripple, unable to relate to themselves, to others, or even to God, in a balanced way. Every experience in life goes through the filter of either the "rejection" personality, which is weak and timid, or the "rebellion" personality, which is angry and aggressive.

Although at this stage, we did not have a lot of

evidence in my own case to go on, this did appear to offer an explanation for the constant changeableness I experienced. Today, a particular situation might cause me much hurt and tears, tomorrow, the very same incident might produce extreme anger and rebellion. With some trepidation, Pastor Richards allowed me to study this material myself. It could help, or it could freak me out completely. Praise the Lord, it did help. At least now I could see there was a pattern to my particular problem, and therefore there would come an end some day. At this point, I had come to feel that my life was just a bottomless sack into which one could dip and call out just about any demon imaginable. In fact, as I studied these pages and read the lists of possible problem areas in the life of a schizophrenic person, I recognised many of them immediately as areas with which I had been struggling for years. It would only be a matter of time before we would know which, if any, were still demonic strongholds. For the moment however, I had peace and rejoiced in the Lord's goodness.

My peace however, was again very short lived. These problems had remained untouched for so many years. Now that the Holy Spirit had begun the work of untangling the emotional and psychological mess that was my internal life, it seemed He would not allow me to rest until it was all done. While still rebuilding the cleansed areas with the Word of God, fellowship and prayer, I soon recognised further demonic reaction within me at our meetings, a churning up and overwhelming blackness within me as I sat under the preaching of the Word of God. At the same time, there arose the possibility that Pastor Richards and Mary may have to move on to pastor another church, and this totally rocked what little security I had. Up to that point I had not realised to what extent I was depending on them and not on God Himself. They had, after all, been the only people who had ever been able to help me, and I began to go to pieces at the thought of losing them. Although they had constantly turned my attention back to the Lord, and counselled me to rebuild my life on Him alone, I had unconsciously grown to depend on them. I now had to look very closely at the root of my insecurity and with God's help begin to shift my dependency back on to Him alone.

I now began to see what was to become a pattern for the future in uncovering demonic activity in my life. First, there would come conviction from the Holy Spirit regarding sin in a particular area. On going before the Lord for clarification He would then open up the areas and ways in which this sin had had effect. Obviously the next step required absolute repentance and renunciation of the sin or attitude, and forgiveness of others where necesary.

Next, came the work of renewing the mind with the Word of God. This I did very systematically. Armed with a concordance and a notebook, I wrote on one page key scriptures regarding that sin – what it was in God's eyes. Learning and meditating on these scriptures drove the conviction deeper and deeper, cutting like a knife, until the abhorrence of it was so great that I could fall completely out of agreement with it. On the opposite page, I noted the scriptures that told me what fruit needed to grow in that area, when the sin was weeded out. For rebellion, there were verses about submission; for hate, love, and so on. (This meant that seeds were already sown, and shooting up even if a demon needed to be cast out of ones life. When the demon was gone, the fruit of the Spirit was already there ready to flourish in the clearer environment, bringing forth fruit meet for repentance.)

The hold of the sin was now broken, and if it was simply a work of the flesh, it would eventually come into line with the Word of God, through the renewing of the mind and will.

If there was a demon present, the Word of God would be now forming a wedge between my own spirit and the evil spirit. The evil spirit would be manifesting now. Not so much in the causing to sin, because the flesh was coming under the control of the Spirit, but as a great burden or extra weight being "evicted" from the body. Until deliverance this could cause great physical and spiritual discomfort, making it very difficult to listen to, or read the Word of God, or enter into worship. Even to concentrate on the ordinary things of life was a battle as one's whole consciousness seemed to be taken up with the conflict within. Although there could be a breakthrough at times to praise and worship God in the spirit, there could be no lasting peace until the demon was at last gone.

So I was back again to studying the Word regarding my security in God. I was soon greatly challenged by the fact that to find security in anyone or anything besides God, is actually unfaithfulness to Him. Job 31:24–28 NIV says "*If I have put my trust in gold or said to pure gold* (or anything else as I understood it) *You are my security . . . then these would be sins to be judged, for I would have been unfaithful to God on high*". On the other hand, God's promises to those who put their trust in Him alone, were everything my heart desired. Yet the Lord asked me very clearly at that time – do you really want to be clear and free? It seemed a strange question, with an obvious answer, and yet God's challenge was clear – insecurity had always caused me to lean on someone. To some extent I had enjoyed needing people – it had been my point of contact, my way of relating. Was I really prepared to let that go now and face the task of learning to relate on an equal level, giving and receiving love, and not just "feeding off" those I leaned on?

Although it was only several weeks since my last deliverance, the pastor agreed to pray with me again, because of the extent of my agitation and anxiety. It is not hard to imagine the amount of pressure these struggles were bringing into our home, as I endeavoured to fulfil the needs of our five children, be the wife I should be, keep the household running somehow, and yet carry this turmoil around with me constantly. Through all these months I was indebted to the Lord for Detlef, who constantly and patiently supported, encouraged, pushed and challenged me to keep pressing on in God regardless of how desperate I felt. Without him challenging me to rise in faith above my problems, many mornings I could not even have left my bed.

Again, in my preparation, the Holy Spirit brought back to my memory the incidents in my childhood which seemed to have opened the door to this spirit, which now caused such problems. There were so many memories of major or minor importance which seemed to linger in the background of my consciousness. Many of these were not of significant events, rather just impressions, and I had often wondered why I remembered these incidents more so than others. I was to find as time went by that many of these incidents were in fact entry points for evil spirits, and as the Lord unfolded the past, layer by layer, they were to connect with sins or hang-ups that were now being dealt with.

This particular incident had happened when as a child I travelled to the country with my friend and family, to deliver her to her brother's farm for her annual holiday. I was to return home the same day with the family. However, as it was approaching time to travel home, somebody decided without consulting me or my parents, that it would be an excellent idea for me to stay for a little holiday as well, and my parents would certainly be delighted for me. I was too little and shy to protest, and so they set off for home without me, leaving me not knowing when I was ever going to see my home again. I was completely unprepared for staying in the country that night. A little girl from Crumlin where the streets were never in darkness, who went to sleep every night to a lullaby of ambulances from the hospital, fire brigade sirens from the local station, and the seemingly endless whirr of C.I.E. buses up and down the main road. As darkness fell on the farm that night, the panic in my stomach rose to meet it, but I somehow managed to control it until bedtime. At that point however, all hell seemed to let loose as I could no longer cope with the strange quietness and isolation of that place. I completely lost control of myself (yet again!) and kicked and screamed and demanded to be brought home. I was so beside myself with fear and trauma that I threatened to run to the village and tell the policeman that these people had kidnapped me. My poor unfortunate hosts were astounded, needless to say, and somehow managed to quieten me down with the promise to drive me home the next day, which they did. I was actually so embarrassed at my own extraordinary behaviour, that I never even spoke to my parents about what had happened, although I am sure they must have been told. They certainly never asked me about it, but perhaps if I could have talked about it, it might not have affected me so deeply for so long. However I had lived my whole life with a very deep but clear sense that out there in the world just about anything could happen to me at any time; that I had no protection from what others might do to me. This insecurity of course meant I could never trust God either, after all He seemed to be part of the great threatening unknown. But now I was learning from the Word that I could trust God to protect me, and the Word had begun to dislodge that spirit of insecurity that had terrified me all my life.

# Chapter Six

The day before I was to come for prayer I had a very strange experience. I had seldom experienced anything that could be remotely described as a "vision" and was rather dubious about such things. As I awoke on this morning, however, in the dim dawn light something caught my attention in the corner of our room. By our bed there stood, not unusually, a bedside lamp. Only this morning as I glanced towards the clock, I saw not the lamp, but a statue I had not seen for many years. This particular statue was one of Mary the Madonna, which had stood on a mantelpiece over my bed all through my childhood. I do not think it had ever even crossed my mind since I had left my parent's home. Obviously, I sat up to take a closer look, but with that, the statue was gone, and I saw only the lamp again. Realising I had probably been dreaming, I joked with my husband – "Do you think the Lord is trying to tell me something about that statue?" but I then put the incident aside. After all, I thought, what could it mean anyway? I had left the Catholic church years ago, and had never had a particular fondness for religious statues or artifacts of any kind. Like most other Irish children of that time, I had gone through the sacraments of Baptism, Holy Communion and Confirmation, but they had never held any real spiritual significance for me. The whole "vision" must have been a figment of my imagination!

You can imagine my amazement then the next day in the prayer time, when this "picture" of the statue returned very clearly to my mind's eye. The spirit of insecurity had been successfully cast out, yet while the team continued to pray, amidst the manifestations within myself, I "saw" a series of images of idols, which even at that moment seemed to be demanding my subservience. The image of the Madonna was one, followed by the picture of the guru to whom I had been dedicated at the initiation ceremony into transcendental meditation. Interrupting the prayer, I explained what was going on inside me, and this was quickly recognised as a manifestation of a religious spirit. It appeared that because as a child I had been dedicated to the Catholic church, the ruling idolatrous spirit still had a claim on me, and tried to influence my life. Of course my life now belonged to Jesus, but until the blood of Jesus had been applied to this area, and any legal hold broken in His Name, this spirit still held its ground. It would have been happy to have me involved in any false religion, such as Yoga, T.M., etc., as long as it kept me from the truth in Jesus. Now exposed and renounced, this deceivers' hold was now broken in the name of Jesus. I was only to discover in the following weeks just how deep had been its influence in my experience.

If the way I felt on that day was anything to go by, I was now completely free, and delivered from the things of the past. For the first time ever I felt incredibly light and joyful. I knew I had much growing to do in God, but it seemed that nothing could stop me now. Only days before, the demons within had suggested that life would be dull and boring without them, that a life of consistency in God would be uneventful and without fun. Now those struggles seemed to be gone forever. I was on top of the world, and I thought myself ready to take on whatever life would bring my way. I had never felt so secure or good about myself before, and could honestly say "The old has gone, the new has come".

By the grace of God, I now had a little respite from the battle, and we all rejoiced together. There was one surprising area that saw immediate change for the better, and that was in the physical side of our marriage. Although we had never had any major problems in this area, we had discussed aspects and attitudes in counselling from time to time. For all my past promiscuity, deep down inside I had quite a puritanical attitude to sex. Although I knew with my mind that what God had created was good, somehow the old "sex is dirty" idea seemed to pervade my thinking, preventing me from enjoying the fulfilment that God had provided for us as a couple. Overnight, that sense of guilt disappeared with the absence of the religious spirit. I began for the first time to enjoy our relationship with a sense of innocence, as something good, healthy and wholesome. I had thought my past would be with me forever, but here the Lord was graciously restoring the years the locusts had eaten, even in this area, and we were amazed.

However, when the euphoria died down and

normality had to be faced, I came down with a bang. Pastor Richards and Mary got on with the business of ministering to the rest of the Fellowship, and I apparently now delivered and free, came face to face with the huge chasm inside. The demons were gone, and yet there was so little experience of God in those areas to replace them. Between the external pressure they were now exerting against me, and my own sense of utter weakness, I thought I would surely crack. I was accustomed to the backlash from these spirits in the wake of deliverance, knowing they would earnestly try to make an inroad in the vulnerable time just after their expulsion. Somehow, I was determined to battle it out alone, and felt that if I ran to the telephone to call for help, I would have given back ground in terms of depending on others. "If I can hold out, if I can hang on to the Lord when I cannot yet sense him in any way in the midst of this wretchedness, if I get through this alone with him, then I can go anywhere with him". I will be free, I told myself. I had always had shallow roots and been a leaning tree; now I had to get my roots down deep, with that "bed-rock" now gone, and some day maybe I could be a strong supporting arm for others. But I had become so accustomed to receiving attention and help to the flesh, I was probably experiencing withdrawal symptoms. No wonder the Lord had asked me "Do you really want to be free"? If I had known how horrendous the battle was going to be, perhaps I never would have started down this road. I was also beginning to see where the religious spirit had played a part in all of this.

These spirits will settle for idolatry in any form, whether in setting up people, possessions, occupations or anything else on the throne that ought to be reserved in ones heart for God alone. Hiding behind an emotional problem, this spirit caused homage to be paid to people, instead of God, and love and appraisal sought from people rather than from God. It was a very subtle and deceptive work.

Disappointed to find continuing difficulty in detaching myself from this inordinate affection for others, I could only press on in the battle to find my own identity and worth in God alone. I knew I had to find my bearings with God as my reference point as a ship at sea would refer to the moon or the sun. To look around me at circumstances or people could bring me no salvation or security, and I had no right to look for more than "brotherly love" from my brothers and sisters. As I read the Word and sought the Lord, little by little revelation and hope began to penetrate the darkness. Ephesians laid out so clearly the enormous lengths God had gone to, to plan and provide for my salvation through his Son, Jesus, even before creation. I could not help but ask "Why?" As I pondered I wrote these notes:-

> "Yes, the plan of Salvation was to display God's own glory and grace, but yet it has begun to dawn on me that perhaps His Father heart longs for my love too. My love cannot add to His power or majesty, and yet, perhaps in a sense He needs and wants me as I need and want Him. The commandment

is to love the Lord your God with your whole heart, with your whole soul and your whole mind. Surely, it was not only out of objective compassion that the Father sent Jesus, but also, because He longed for reciprocated freely given love from us, from me. What a thought that the God of heaven might really want and desire my love, attention and affection. If that is so, then, yes Lord, you can have my love.

I have come to see that there are two sides to rejection – the one is that nobody loves me, but the other is that nobody wants my love. If in God complete healing can be found, then it must be true that He loves me, and that He wants and values my love too. Lord, if this is true, reveal it deep within my spirit I pray, and make this a new day in my experience with you".

# Chapter Seven

"Witchcraft" – at the sound of the word something erupted inside me. Something violent, destructive and hateful. It was only one week later, and yet the conflict between the truth that God was bringing into my life, and the demanding possessiveness that drove me, had risen to such proportions, that I was now back in the ministry room again. We paused to reappraise the situation. The Holy Spirit had led the Pastor to pray against this spirit, but I was horrified at my reaction – how could witchcraft be a part of my life? It was then I recalled that scene my mother had so often referred to, the gypsy in Canada who had apparently foreseen so much of what did actually happen in our family. Was it possible that her reference to me, and my mother's acceptance of her words, had made a way for this spirit to influence my life? Had it dogged my footsteps all through my life, seeking to do its damage? The ensuing battle was truly a conflict between heaven and hell until this controlling spirit of witchcraft was eventually cast out, spewing out threats of murder and destruction. As it was leaving, I saw in my spirit our little Fellowship, the faces of my brothers and sisters, and knew without doubt that this spirit had been commissioned to destroy them. I could sense and feel the fear and disgrace of this spirit, as it was now being cast out and its work thwarted. It would have to go back to face its master as a failure, overcome by the blood of Jesus.

The implications of what we had discovered, just about wiped me out completely. Here I had been so active and so committed a member of our Fellowship, I had thought I was being helpful and supportive, wanting to see it established in God. Yet all along, there had been something inside me influencing me, driving me, trying to use me to destroy. I remembered with horror so many situations in which I had expressed my strong opinions, trying perhaps unconsciously to influence the leading of the Fellowship and its direction, out of the will of God. Perhaps that was why I had always got alongside the leadership in situations in the past, befriending them, but trying to control them? Perhaps that was why it was always so important to me to know all that was going on in the Fellowship? In the spirit realm, was information being fed back into hell, adding to its strategy for squeezing the life out of the Christian church? And was "control" the reason why I always needed to feel involved at the hub of Christian situations?

Perhaps even more painful to face was the knowledge that this spirit had obviously also been working within our home, to keep my marriage, husband and children from ever being all they were meant to be in God. In the arrogance of my heart, I had always thought of myself as brighter, more spiritual and infinitely wiser than my husband. I saw myself as the leader of the field, constantly pushing, pulling and cajoling him into shape. Now I realised I had simply been trying to control him, and was actually hindering him. No wonder he had so often resisted my efforts which I thought were so well intentioned.

He had known instinctively that what I was doing was out of order, and was actually smothering him. As I looked around me, from what I now knew, I began to see that mine was not an isolated demonic problem, but that control played a major role in the structure of our matriarchal society. Controlling mothers whose grown sons were afraid of living their own lives. So many fearful, downtrodden men, with manipulative wives, who were most certainly the power behind the throne, Christian or otherwise.

I had now to put my own house in order of course, and take an honest look at my relationship with my own children. I had never felt I had been over possessive with them, or even over strict with them. Yet, now I felt somehow different towards them, freer and more separate from them in a healthy way. I saw that often my discipline of them was not so much to teach them aright, but rather from the attitude of "how dare they disobey me"? I saw that I had tried to control their father's relationship with them. When he disciplined them I complained, when he did not discipline them I complained. I seemed to be constantly trying to defend them, protect them, speak for him, and generally interfere with their relationships. It was as if I were trying to block any real influence he might have in the family, and I thought this was all for our good. Over time I was to learn how to relax and begin to live within God's ordained order, knowing that He would bless our relationship as I let go and trusted Him to lead and direct our family through the head of the home, my husband.

It would stand to reason, that exerting such control over people and situations took a great deal of physical effort, living out of a false strength. This in turn led to much physical tension and often recurring migraine headaches and sinus problems. With the spirit of control now out of my life, these diminished greatly and over time have disappeared completely. I certainly was being purified "spirit, soul and body".

However, before I was to know all the blessing and fruit of freedom from this spirit, the immediate days following my deliverance had first to be faced. I waited for the sense of hateful violence to settle down within me, but I waited in vain. With each passing day, the aggressive and destructive tendency grew stronger until I became afraid of what I might do. Yes, control was gone, but it seemed some of its cohorts had been stirred up. Coming to terms with what had been discovered in my life definitely did not come easily. I had always regarded myself as a fairly normal person with a few hang-ups. Now, although I knew I was so much better for having had deliverance, I began to feel I had lost my grip on normality altogether. I looked at the other women in my position in the Fellowship, who had not needed deliverance, and thought "I will never catch up on them now, I will never be as good, I have gone too far back down this road". Instead of going on in God, I appeared to be going deeper into the pit; although the Word said "*unless a grain of wheat falls into the earth and dies, it remains alone*". (John 12:24 RSV) The dying was proving extremely painful. All my aspirations towards ever serving God were becoming more elusive, as the enemy told me no one would ever trust me after all I had told them about myself. Yet there was no other real way ahead, but to try to stop comparing myself with others. However much of a freak I thought I was, God must surely have a plan for my life too, and eventually I would have to accept God's right as the potter to deal with my life in his sovereignty.

Through the week, my aggravation grew. I could not listen to worship music without screaming with anger, and even the sight of a Bible made me want to fling it into the fire. I literally felt like killing somebody. "Keep your head down and keep busy" I was counselled, and I spent the next days cleaning the house and vacuuming it from top to bottom, trying not to get drawn into the children's squabbles for fear of over-reacting. Seeing no improvement with time, it was agreed to pray for me again after our Thursday meeting. It was one week since the last ministry. By the grace of God alone I got through the meeting, standing next to the wall just to hold myself up. The music group played just a few feet in front of me. The young guitarist will never know how close he came to being assaulted with his own guitar, such was the violence raging inside me. At last we came to prayer. I was experiencing the clearest sense of dual identity within that I had ever had. The real me loved and respected Pastor Richards;

the demons within hated him and his authority, and were screaming for his blood.

In desperation I asked Mary to take my high heeled shoes away as I was afraid I might not be able to control the urge to kill him. In the hours that followed Pastor and the team wrestled with these spirits of hatred, murder and violence. How had they become strongholds in my heart? I knew myself they were connected with my old lost love, upon whom I had threatened revenge some day. The Holy Spirit had again put His finger on the poisonous root of the problem, and had begun to squeeze. Could I again forgive? Could I let go now of hatred and revenge? Could I humble myself and seek forgiveness for my own evil attitudes buried so deeply all these years? The heart is indeed deceitful and exceedingly wicked. Through the mercy of God and the patient perseverance of the ministry team, these spirits were eventually expelled from my life that night.

But there was even deeper work to be done. What about those areas of my own heart? of my own "self" that had accommodated these feelings of revenge? What was it that allowed me to feel I had the right to such hatred? Out of the depths of my being the Lord called the spirits of self-pity, self-love, even self-worship. Those spirits which had pandered to the desires of my own heart, when nobody else seemed to care. They had locked me into selfish desires, and had made it impossible for me to really love myself or others with a godly love.

By the early hours of the morning the battle was over and with a truly grateful heart I could thank God for the gift of this ministry of deliverance to the body of Christ; for the power and authority of the name and the blood of Jesus, and for the brothers and sisters who cared enough to spend these hours in spiritual warfare on my behalf. I had certainly been the recipient of God's great mercy and grace.

# Chapter Eight

We were now entering a very busy time within the Fellowship. To our great joy, the first phase of our church building, The Bray New Life Centre, was nearing completion, and all the members were enthusiastically joining "paint-ins" and work parties. It was an ideal time to be rebuilding one's life, as the opportunities for fellowship and interaction with brothers and sisters were endless. It was ideal too from the point of view that what was happening within our building, complete refurbishment and restoration, was such a clear allegory for what was now happening in so many of our lives. Over the months, many more people had come to realise their own need for deliverance, and it was encouraging for myself, to be able to testify to God's wonderful ability to solve the unsolvable. Our Pastor was teaching a Bible study series on "Nehemiah" and the rebuilding of the walls of Jerusalem. Nehemiah's statement of faith became our watchword "*The God of Heaven will grant us success*".

I myself was ticking the days off the calendar, measuring the success of my deliverance. One week and still holding – two weeks and still holding! Three weeks and still holding! I was now knowing a consistency in my emotions that was quite unlike the old me, and I felt at last I had come off that emotional carousel. With the extreme of the hard-hitting, rebellious side of my personality now dealt with, I could begin to feel that maybe I did have a heart of flesh after all. Although, yet far from perfect, I sensed little saplings of love starting to flourish and nervously reach out to others. More than ever, I could now appreciate my husband and children for who they were as individuals, and begin to enjoy them, laugh at their jokes, share in their fun without the constant pressure of my own problems. With a growing intercession ministry now firmly established within the Fellowship, I found I was now able to make more of my heart available for the Lord's burden in prayer. So much of my time and attention had been swallowed up in simply coping with myself.

It was sitting under the revelation preaching of the Word of God in Nehemiah, that began to stir up the next "layer" of spirits that the Holy Spirit had decided to deal with. So much of Israel's problem and defeat had been caused by their close association in the past with foreign gods. This had led to a large occupation of their nation by their enemy, carried down into succeeding generations.

Just as Israel had to rid themselves of everything pertaining to foreign gods, we were encouraged to look closely at our own lives and rid ourselves of anything physical or spiritual that could yet hold us in bondage to the enemy. I was beginning to recognise again something inside reacting uncomfortably to the Word of God. I began to go through my life and our cupboards with a fine tooth comb; anything dubious that was uncovered was destroyed. Photographs, letters, documents, anything that I felt had any association with anything ungodly in the past, went in the fire. Prayers that were embedded in my memory since childhood; an "innocent" blood covenant I had made with a childhood friend; all of these were renounced and any wrong attachment cut off by the blood of Jesus. I was not going to take any chances in the area of giving legal ground to the enemy.

Although I seemed to take the Word of God in, walk in it and apply it, over and over again in my heart I was hearing these days the words – "an evil heart of unbelief", "an evil heart of unbelief". Could I have such a spirit? I asked the Lord. I had now become so sufficiently objective about demons that I could deliberately work at "tormenting" them out of hiding. If there was a spirit of unbelief working in my life, faith was the obvious antidote. I began to fast and pray, to study the Word on faith, listen to tapes, do everything I could to press in on any demons, and eventually I got results. In time, I felt the angry reaction of this spirit to the word of faith, and I knew it could be only a matter of time before I would be free of it.

In the meantime, I was to learn a lot about faith, since because of our building project it would yet be some weeks before I could have ministry. Meanwhile, something strange and very frightening had begun to occur in my mind. Throughout all of the turmoil of preparation and deliverance, while I had so often felt emotionally devastated, I had been able to keep my mind under control, to a reasonable extent. Somehow,

I had managed to stay on top of what was happening to me. But now it was different. At any unexpected moment, I could sense what felt like an icy hand crawling over my brain, its steely fingers locking my mind in its grip and literally taking me captive. "You are going to go mad" it threatened in my mind; "you will lose control and then all the others (demons) can come back again".

This was recurring over and over again, in my dreams, driving the car, doing the housework, until I became terrified with the idea that so much deliverance would actually drive me mad. Perhaps I could not take it; pehaps I would crack up and eventually be locked up. If ever I needed the constant reassurance of those around me, it was now. As the time of deliverance grew closer, the battle became more intense. In those moments, all I could do was to cry out to the Lord for help, and fight to hold on to reality. How could I stay in faith for deliverance if I could not even apply my mind to the Word of God. It was in this time, I began to see that faith is not a product of the mind at all. My mind was being renewed by the Word of God, but faith was birthed within my born-again spirit, which no demon could control. This meant that when that awful sense of insanity overtook my mind, although it fought a determined battle, I could still withdraw within my spirit and in there hide myself in God. It was only the knowledge that this was possible that kept me from going over the brink, until that spirit of insanity was eventually expelled from my mind.

Several weeks later, this spirit was indeed dealt with along with the spirit of unbelief, as I had suspected. I thanked God for the preaching of faith among us, as without it I would never have known I had an unbelieving spirit. As a result of the work of cutting off the past, other spirits inherited from previous generations were also cast out that day. I should have gone home rejoicing, but I did not.

Although we had spent hours struggling with these strong spirits, still I knew I was not free. What was gone, was gone, but there was yet more stirred up. I went home feeling dead inside – depressed, hopeless. When would I ever be free? What had I done to bring so many evil spirits into my life? How does anyone get so bad, so demonised? By that evening the sense of despair drove me to the point of wanting to lie down and die. I talked to Pastor Richards. I could not as a Christian commit suicide, could I? Then I would surely go to hell. But I just would not, could not go on living like this anymore. Deliverance had been my only hope, now it seemed even that had failed to completely dispel the darkness inside. Obviously, I could not be left in that condition, and it was agreed to meet me again the next evening. That was the blackest night I had ever experienced. I hated myself for ever being such a hopeless, horrible creature, for all the things I had been and done. Death itself seemed to be the only escape. I awoke in the night, desperately needing a drink. The darkness was so oppressive and terrifying that I could only crawl to the bathroom on my hands and knees, crying out to the Lord for help – "You said you would never leave me nor forsake me". Only by his grace and his hand upon me did I manage to get through to our arranged meeting.

Without further ado, these strong negative spirits were addressed. First, they had to be addressed and renounced by me. I had never fully understood the power of our own words and confession until the moment when I had to declare in faith to the spirit of self hate, "I do not hate myself". All my life I had been hating myself and putting myself down constantly with the words of my own mouth. Now I had to fall out of agreement with this spirit and confess my agreement with what the Word of God said about me. Until I could do that, this spirit did not have to leave. As we prayed I recalled all the hopeless, depressive music I had listened to throughout my youth. The blues music, the soul music – so much of what I had filled my spirit with had fed these spirits of hopelessness, suicide and death which were now trying to take over and destroy my life. They had taken advantage of the heartbreak of the past, and built a stronghold for themselves in my soul.

Although exhausted after days of ministry to others, the ministry team pressed in and on until every one of these death-producing spirits were cast out. They had learned with time, that while there may be one specific ruling spirit in a particular area, there could also be a number of other lesser spirits, unnamed and unknown, also at work as part of that group of demons. This time they were careful to keep on going until all rulers and their underlings were gone. At last the spirit of hopelessness was leaving. I could feel it so clearly being pushed up out of the depths of my being.

Behind it was rising the joy of the Lord, seeming almost to evict it. As it left I shouted for joy, startling all those around me. They were exhausted and feared the worst – was there more to come? But, no, the transformation was hard to believe but it was true. I had come in to that room depressive and suicidal, now I was going home brimming over with joy and love, and was so glad to be alive. Glory to God.

After nine deliverance sessions in just seven months, the summer came as a time of welcome relaxation and refreshment. With the restoration of the first phase of our building complex now complete, many members of the Fellowship took off for a well earned holiday. As some left and visitors arrived, the spiritual environment tended to be less intense for some weeks, and it would be unlikely that I should experience any major problems for a while. Time now to enjoy all that God had so graciously done in the year past and to continue to rebuild and retrain. Our Pastor and his wife would be away for some time combining conferences and holidays, and this would be an opportunity to prove to what extent I had been building into God alone, rather than into people.

Perhaps one of the most difficult things to achieve during this whole process of deliverance was detachment from those who were helping me, and dependence on God alone as my all in all. 2 Peter 1 verse 3 NIV says "*His divine power has given us everything we need for life and godliness*". So often the flesh would long for attention or reassurance, but I would have to keep coming back to that verse, knowing that it must be possible for me to find everything I need, physically, spiritually and emotionally in Jesus Himself. It was so necessary for my counsellors to stand back sufficiently from me, to ensure that I did not become dependent on them. Otherwise the whole objective of restoring and establishing me in God would have been lost.

With so much of my personality now having been dismantled, I began to feel a little like the children's T.V. character, the "Bionic Man" who was once blown apart and put back together again, with an inbuilt super power. Certainly I was finding a power for living that I had never been able to experience before. Now that so many destructive forces were gone from my life obviously my disposition became much more cheerful and positive. There had also been many fears and anxieties related to areas which had been demonised, and I was now knowing freedom from fear for the first time in my life. It was only now as I found myself so much freer to enjoy my husband and family, that I realised just how incapacitating my problems had been.

There was only one thing that bothered me – somewhere along the way I seemed to have lost whatever creative ability I had had for the childrens' ministry. I was not quite sure whether it had been demonic ability which I had "lost" with the demons, or whether I was just exhausted. Whichever was the case, I did have a growing conviction that my days with the children were drawing to a close.

# Chapter Nine

It had always amazed me how the Holy Spirit used the very ordinary situations of life to expose the deeply rooted problems I had, and this period proved to be no exception. While our pastor was away during the summer months, we had a number of visiting speakers. Although we had a good strong leadership team taking care of the congregation, I was feeling spiritually a little insecure, with our "covering ministry" absent. Anything that I heard preached which was not quite in line with what I was accustomed to, really disturbed me. I began to realise that I was quite paranoid about "the truth" and not for altogether healthy reasons. Reading through the book of Galatians, I realised that although I did not work at keeping the law for my salvation, certainly staying in the truth was a law and a bondage for me. I was terrified of being deceived, of falling short in my faith, that somehow if I did not have every jot and tittle of my doctrine right, God might bring judgement crashing down on my head. There was really no room in my thinking in this area for the grace of God. This was simply perfectionism as a "works mentality" translated into matters of faith and doctrine. Anyone who has tried to live up to the self inflicted standard of the perfectionist knows the crippling guilt and the deep sense of unworthiness and failure that inevitably result.

There is no room or allowance made for one's own weakness or humanity, and the fact that God might make allowances for our frailty, in His mercy and grace towards us, is beyond comprehension.

It soon became clear to me, that because I had been unable to accept my less than perfect self, I had slipped over to the other extreme of pride, in order to compensate. I had become "puffed up" in order to cover up. Soon our Bible School was to open and I enrolled with great enthusiasm. Here at last was the opportunity to reclaim some of the lost years of my education. I would be the star pupil and everyone would acknowledge how wonderfully clever, intelligent and spiritual I was. It was not long before the Holy Spirit tripped me up with my own base motives, and I was forced to admit again how deceitful and wicked my heart was. I thought I was living for God's glory, but really it was my own ego and pride that motivated me.

I was thus persuaded that I again needed help and ministry, and when Pastor Richards and Mary returned from their annual leave, I greeted them with all the Lord had been showing me. After several weeks of observing the enormous spiritual pressure and frustration I was experiencing, they agreed to pray with me again. I came, assuming everything would be simple and straight forward. They would pray, I would get delivered, we would all go home, and everything would be fine. However, it just did not work out like that. Whether because of what I was dealing with, or because of lack of clarity or preparation on my part, this session was disastrous.

Yes, I did get delivered of the things I had confessed and acknowledged. Yet, even after several hours, I was still so disturbed and discouraged. I lost sight of all that God had already done for me, and began to wonder aloud if any of this was worthwhile at all. Not surprisingly, this brought me a stern rebuke from the Pastor to the effect that to speak like that was opening myself to the enemy again. I had better get back into faith and thank God again for His goodness to me. That rebuke absolutely shattered me. The only thing I had ever done successfully in my whole life was to get delivered, by cooperating with the Lord and those ministering to me. Now I felt I had failed even at that. Worse still was the sense of having disappointed and discouraged those people who had expended so much time and energy on my behalf. They would surely give up on me now and reject me like all the others.

I went home and cried for weeks. With the spirit of pride gone, the curtain had been drawn on my real self. In pride, there had been the ability to be all that I was and yet not face it. I could say, "I may do what others do, but inside I am not really as bad as them". Now the knowledge of my absolute selfishness and God's longsuffering with me completely overwhelmed me.

The demonic stronghold of my own "self', my own ego, had now been torn down, and I found myself temporarily without motivation to go on with life. At heart, I had been living for myself all these years. Mixed with my desire to serve

God had been the question of "What is in it for me?" Now there was no grasping for self, but I had not yet learned how to live for God. I was in a limbo and could not see myself ever getting out of this nothingness. Would I even have the will to go on in deliverance until I was completely free?

Yet the Holy Spirit reminded me that the Word of God is "*quick and powerful . . . dividing asunder soul and spirit*" (Hebrews 4:12 AV). If I could stay in the Word, read it, study it and rest in God, in time it would do its own work of separation in my life. It would uncover any demon at work there. Sooner or later, I would be free.

It was probably significant in the sovereignty of God, that having been delivered of a "perfectionist" spirit, the first thing I should have to contend with would be supposed failure. In time I did come to terms with what had happened. In the past, correction and discipline had always meant rejection. My feeling was "If you really love me, why do you not just accept me the way I am?" At last a breakthrough came when I read again the words in Hebrews 12:6 NIV – "*The Lord disciplines those he loves, and he punishes everyone he accepts as a son*". Realising that Pastor's correction was because he and God loved me and wanted to get me back on course, I could now accept it. For the first time in my life, I could actually thank God for my husband and those in authority over me as God's provision for me, who would take care of me, and help to keep me on the "straight and narrow". I was so thankful for God's love that accepts me the way I am but loves me enough not to leave me that way.

At last I was crawling out of the cave I had been buried in for weeks. My attitude slowly came around again to one of positive faith and victory and a determination again to pursue my enemies into the dust. With so many emotional and psychological areas of my life already having been cleansed and delivered by the blood of Jesus, I had made up my mind that time was up for whatever was left. Now that I could observe myself more objectively, I began to work systematically through any area and any sin of which I became aware. I was ruthless, relentless and repentant of anything the Holy Spirit brought to my attention. Jealousy and mistrust of others still caused me much heartache. I knew that to be jealous of others was an affront to God's very nature of love, which values each of us equally and shows no favouritism. When God loves me so completely and unconditionally, why should I ever need to worry about what he is doing with others. Nothing can diminish His love for me.

It had been mentioned to me of late that perhaps my eating habits might warrant some attention, but initially I resisted vehemently any suggestion that perhaps I had a difficulty with food. I was quite thin, but then I was a busy mother of five young children, and as far as I was aware, I ate plenty and often. However, I agreed to seek the Lord about the matter, and observe my own behaviour as much as possible. What I observed quite disturbed me. The first thing I discovered was my inability to eat in public. After a meeting one day I was standing with a cup of coffee and a half eaten biscuit in my hand, when a visitor stopped to talk with me. Suddenly I realised I felt embarrassed and could almost hear myself thinking "if she notices me eating this biscuit, she will think no wonder you are so fat, gorging yourself like that". The point was I was not fat at all, approximately eight stone in weight, at 5′4″ in height. There certainly had been a time when I was fat, before I had become a Christian. Between drinking and overeating I had been decidedly round, and my eating habits certainly would have embarrassed me if they had been discovered. However, all of that excess weight had been shed with a very strict diet when I got saved, but it was clear that subconsciously I was still "thinking" fat and seeing myself as fat.

It also began to come home to me the many days in the past when I had found it impossible to eat. So often I would have cooked a good meal for the family, and sat down with them feeling really ravenous. Yet, after two or three mouthfuls of food, I would begin to feel nauseous and seldom if ever finished a proper meal. I had always put this down to exhaustion or just a natural loss of appetite, so I decided to force myself to eat, just to see what would happen. Strangely, the more I went against my feelings of repulsion, the stronger they seemed to get; it was soon apparent that there was something deeper influencing my attitude to food. As I went back before the Lord about this whole matter, my thoughts were drawn back to my old habits of over-indulgence. For some inexplicable reason I had always carried in my memory a particular night, when on returning home disturbed and depressed after a disastrous night out, I sat down and gorged and comforted myself with whatever niceties I could find in the kitchen cupboard. I had always wondered why I recalled that night so vividly, and now asked the Lord, "Did I say 'yes' to gluttony that night?" Yet why could I not eat now?

If that memory held any significance, then that led me to another issue, for there was another incident of apparently equal unimportance, yet it too was clearly stamped on my memory. I could recall lying in bed one Saturday morning as a child of perhaps ten or eleven years old. Obviously there was no school to attend and my mother had gone shopping. I was enjoying a long lie-in, snuggled up in bed with my "Mary-Lou of the Chalet School" book. I remembered at one point being concious of the thought – "it is really very late, I probably should get up". After a moment's consideration, I said "No, I like it better here," and stretching out to enjoy the warmth of the bed, I self-indulgently chose to stay put.

I was now having to ask the Lord again, "Why do I remember that particular day so vividly?" I had probably spent many mornings in such a way. Did something happen, had I opened myself to laziness in a new way? I recalled how angry I had felt some years before when a friend had accused me of being lazy. I saw myself as being a very busy and active person, I had to be, I had a family to take care of. Yet I had to admit there were many days when as much as I loved the children, I dreaded them coming home from school for all the extra demands they would make on me. I never had made any claims to actually enjoying my work at home – give me a good book to read any day – but surely that was just because I was not that type of person. But then there were those occasions when I found it almost physically impossible to get out of my chair and apply myself to my home. I did it of course, because I had to, but I did so often feel there was something literally pushing against me, as I tried to rise up over my flesh. Often tasks which could actually be completed relatively quickly, became a major enterprise for me, and I could not even approach them unless I was psyched up with the assurance that I had plenty of time and plenty of energy to complete them. Could all of this signify the presence of a spirit of laziness, or was I just getting paranoid about demons?

On I went, examining everything with a fine toothcomb. No, I was not being introspective and looking for problems within me. But anything which was causing me a problem of any degree came under the Holy Spirit's spotlight. One thing I had learned through these months was how demons hide within our thoughts and feelings by using the personal pronoun "I". A resident spirit of rejection does not whisper in one's ear, "nobody loves you." If it did so, so impersonally, we might more quickly recognise it as coming from the enemy. But no, a demon will sit within and complain "nobody loves *me*". The person accepts this as their own thought and their own feeling, and is overcome by it. The person really thinks now "nobody loves me" as they go on believing the lie. So many people's patterns of thought and feelings are contrary to the Word of

God, and like myself in the past they might argue "but that is just the way I am, I cannot change that". Often the thought or feeling has originated with the enemy, and they are in fact defending the stand of demons. We need to look very objectively at our thinking patterns and learn to take every thought captive to Christ.

# Chapter Ten

At last the day was set for what I hoped again would be my last session of deliverance. I fasted and prayed and made absolutely certain that my attitude was humble and right before God. I did not want a repetition of the last disaster! The Lord Himself had been very gracious in helping me to prepare by speaking to me in prophecy the week before. He indicated to me that He was going to lead me into a ministry of intercession, and assured me that He would break every power arrayed against me in order that I might do His will. With that promise tucked away in my heart, I came confident in God that He would deliver me. It was exactly one year since I had first set foot down the road to deliverance, the most traumatic but fruitful year of my life.

In I arrived with a wide sweeping "shopping list" for Pastor. Anything that had ever been in the past an area of bondage to me I asked him to pray into, to make sure there would be nothing hidden. In the past, I had certainly been addicted to cigarettes and heavily into alcohol. Blasphemies had tripped off my tongue with great ease. I was again experiencing great apprehension and fear. Everything, upon which the Holy Spirit had been shining His light, I shared, and we went to prayer, relying entirely on this Holy Spirit for His leading.

In the hours that followed, it was my great joy to be set free from many remaining tormentors. At last the spirits of jealousy and mistrust were prised from my personality. As I suspected, addiction, alcoholism and laziness had to be dealt with along with much fear, and blasphemous, railing spirits. Eventually we came down to the self indulgent spirit of gluttony, and it was cast out uncovering as it went, its ally, the anorexic spirit of compulsive starvation. It left, but not before it had made it very plain that its intention had been to kill me. What a victorious morning that was! That evening for the first time in so many years, I sat down to the family meal, and "wiped the platter clean". In the months and situations that followed I found any "hang-up" I had about food disappeared without trace. I have been able to eat disciplined well balanced meals and even managed to gain a little weight. Even at social functions I have been able to eat my fill without hindrance or embarrassment. Perhaps more than any other spirit, the deliverance from anorexia has been the one which draws the most humble gratitude from my heart to God. It had been such a hidden deceptive enemy, trying to destroy me without my realising it. If I had not had Jesus living within me it could well have overtaken me years before, and perhaps like so many other unfortunate young women I would have lost the battle against it. But His power had kept me, and prevented it from having its full way with me until this day when He would set me free from its grip completely. I give Him all the praise and glory that He is due.

With laziness no longer a part of me, it was now

so much easier to keep busy, and tackling those once dreaded tasks became simply routine. With some trepidation I returned to the Fellowship situations where I would have normally experienced such fear of rejection and jealousy. I arrived the first evening and waited. Nothing happened inside. People arrived, conversations were engaged, greetings exchanged, and all the while I waited. Would I feel it again? Would I see something, would somebody say something that would disturb this peace inside, would I feel that dreaded knocking on the inside of me that said "all is not well with my soul". But it did not come. The evening proceeded normally and by the end I realised I had hardly even noticed what was happening between other people. I had been able to relate quite freely to the people I met, and what went on around me did not really matter at all. There was no jealousy, no threat, no fear, just me and the Lord, and the brothers and sisters whom he had given me to love and serve. It was a tremendous freedom, which was to grow and strengthen in the months ahead, as I grew more confident of who I was in God, and could appreciate others in the same way. As I learned to walk in love, I found that yes, hurts and misunderstandings could and would arise between people, but with forgiveness and trust as a God-given "cushion" against life's ill, these situations did not have to cause any lasting damage again. The Living Bible says "*Love does not even notice when it is offended*". Many times since I have had to smile in amazement when people have come and apologised to me for perhaps offending me through some situation and I have realised I had not even noticed, never mind been offended by what had happened. Truly the love of God is shed abroad in our hearts and ready to blossom when all the hindrance is removed.

In the days that immediately followed this latest deliverance my emotional and psychological peace was tremendous. I knew that I was now emotionally free and well on the road to recovery as a whole person. However, that new well-up and flow of the Holy Spirit within me which I had expected did not seem to be coming. I was peaceful, with no disturbances in my spirit, and yet I felt almost dead inside. For some time I had felt what was even physically like a stone slab weighing down on my chest, cold and dead. I could not explain it and could hardly describe it, but when we were together for prayer the next week, I mentioned it to our Pastor. There had been need to pray into one last area, but even then the sensation did not leave me.

"Perhaps that is just normal for me" I suggested. "Perhaps it is nothing to worry about at all". Not realising there was any connection, as we sat chatting, I began to share with the others how drawn I had felt recently to go and visit my mother's grave. Since we now lived so far away, it had been a long time since I had been there, and for some weeks now I had an uncanny desire to go and take the children with me to the cemetery. We talked about Irish people's fascination with graveyards and the dead. Even as we shared, death seemed to become more and more attractive to me, and I could sense myself becoming more passive and numb inside, as I sat there. Death seemed to be drawing me into itself.

Pastor started to pray. "*The cords of death entangled me*" (Psalm 116:3 NIV) "*I will not die but live, and will proclaim what the Lord has done*". (Psalm 118:17 NIV) These were Scriptures the Holy Spirit had brought back to my memory the previous day, and I had not understood why. We realised now they were the "ammunition" with which to fight this battle. Led by the Holy Spirit, Pastor Richards began to address what was actually a familiar spirit. This is a spirit which attaches itself to a person through their connection with some form of occult. It usually identifies itself very closely with the person, even taking on their name. This spirit answered to the name of my mother. They like to stay within families, being passed on from one generation to the next. This spirit had obviously been fed down to me, and was now trying to tighten its grip on my life, by supposedly bringing me back into contact with my dead mother. As the prayer proceeded, somewhere in my distant consciousness I was aware of this spirit howling like a legendary banshee, and then with a sudden terrifying scream, it left me. I could breathe again, my body was light and I was free. Praise the Lord.

I even more fully appreciated the Lord's sovereignty and timing in this matter, when only two days later it was necessary for us to attend a funeral at the very cemetery in question. I was so glad to be able to go in peace, now cleansed and protected by the blood of Jesus.

The absence of this familiar spirit brought

around some extraordinary changes in my life. It seemed as if I had come out of a fog into a clear sunny atmosphere, as I began to see and notice things around me as never before. The beauty of nature, colours and detail seemed to catch my attention wherever I went. The behaviour of one of our children improved dramatically with the cutting off of this spirit, and we could only conclude that this child was marked in the spirit world to inherit it, and was already being oppressed by it. We thank God for His graciousness to us and to our family. I had often had rather dubious experiences in the past, things which I could not quite describe as psychic or of the Holy Spirit, things such as knowing who was calling on the telephone before I answered it, talking about something, and then seeing it actually happen. These were minor things by psychic standards, but nevertheless they never occurred again after this spirit was sent out of me.

# Chapter Eleven

Now Christmas had come round again, and I could truly look back on a year in which God had achieved amazing things on my behalf. Psalm 30:5 (NIV) says, "*Weeping may remain for a night, but rejoicing comes in the morning*". It had been a very long night, but now the tears were dried and the new year beckoned, promising joy and hope in God. As the Lord had indicated, I moved out of the Sunday School work and into the leading of the intercession group of the Fellowship. I had always realised how important this work with the children was, and often asked how the Lord or our leadership could trust me with them, in spite of all my difficulties. Obviously, they had kept a very close eye on how I had handled the children, and by the grace of God there had been no adverse effects in the Sunday School. On the contrary, I had and still have a very good relationship with the children and was very sad to leave them.

Having been the beneficiary of so much ministry in the past year, I was enthusiastic about getting more involved in the battle of light against darkness, in intercession. I had experienced first hand the victory of the name and the blood of Jesus against every enemy. The first Irish Apostolic Training School opened with a very encouraging number of students and we settled down to studying the Word of God with new vigour.

The entrance of your Word brings light, the Scripture says, and now with so many blockages removed from my life, the Word of God was able to enter and bring light and revelation into areas once hidden in darkness. We had always been taught that "revelation requires a response" and so I endeavoured to respond and make adjustments to my life in accordance with the Word that was expounded to us.

The flesh does not always take willingly to making such adjustments, but before long I was finding a resistance in me that went far beyond the flesh. I had no idea of what the problem could be now. Emotionally I was steady and relating well to others. Yet I was again finding authority very hard to take. Since I had been delivered of the other rebellious and defiant spirits, I had been careful to keep my heart attitude right and not allow any room for the enemy to regain ground. I was fairly sure therefore that nothing that had been cast out had in fact re-entered by my indulging in sin. As I sought the Lord and shared my situation with Pastor Richards, we considered the possibilities. It was evident from the Word of God that there is a chain of command, a hierarchy within the underworld, of powers, principalities, and princes as we read in the Book of Daniel. Jesus Himself told of the need to bind the "strong man" before his house could be plundered. It was possible that although so many demons had been cut off from my life, the ruler of some or all of them could still have access and influence. I went before the Lord asking Him for revelation again on these definitely anti-authority feelings I was now dealing with. Months ago I had been delivered of the spirit of rebellion which had influenced me since childhood. This had been the result of the rejection I lived with, but that scenario no longer applied, where there was now no rejection, there was no need for rebellion. The Holy Spirit now brought my thoughts forward to those incidents in my older teens when I was so aggressively defiant towards my parents. Had I somehow compounded the foothold of the enemy in my life when I made these choices as a young adult? I saw now that without excuse and without blame I needed now as an adult to accept the responsibility for my own sin of rebellion before God. "Against thee and thee only have I sinned". I confessed these things as I met with the ministry team to pray. By the grace of God the battle which ensued although very difficult, was successful, as the strong ruling spirit of Anti-christ, the ruler of all lawlessness, anger and rebellion was cast out in the name of Jesus. The spiritual and physical strength of the ruling princes give some indication of their power and authority, but not even the strongest of them can hold out against the powerful blood of Jesus.

I came home remembering little of what had happened, but very conscious that an era of my life, in time and experience had been eradicated. I was aching and tired, and not a little nervous of any further spiritual warfare.

I would now have to wait on God to put me back on my spiritual feet again. In the week that followed I continued to experience extreme conflict and fear regarding intercession and spiritual warfare. However, I was not too sure whether I was afraid of demons or of God. With an outreach meeting arranged in that week, our little group of intercessors had their instructions from the Lord as to how to pray in preparation. With all of this inner conflict how was I to stand before a group of women and encourage and lead them in this battle? Everything within me that morning screamed at me to run away, but with Pastor's counsel not to let the enemy rule the day, I stood my ground. With the prayer support of those closest to me, the grace of God prevailed proving again that "*Greater is He that is in us than he who is in the world*". As we battled together in prayer that morning, the Lord gave us great victory and liberty, assuring us that our prayer had been effective.

However, it was clear that I continued to be very troubled in spirit and I asked Pastor Richards to pray for me again. I was now getting desperate, and no longer cared how, where or with whom, I got delivered. Time was dragging on, and I was getting very discouraged notching up the number of deliverance sessions I had had, and the incredible number of demons that had had access to my life. Then the Holy Spirit encouraged me in His own peculiar way. "Well, even if you add up all the demons you have had, named and unnamed, it still does not make a Legion!". The reference was to the Gadarene man in Mark 5 who had been "possessed" of a Legion of demons, a Legion being 3,000 in number! I had to admit, I certainly had not had that many to contend with, neither had I been demon-possessed, which means that the person is completely over-run and ruled by demons. To be demonised, as I had been, meant simply that particular areas of the soul or body had been under the influence of demons. I took the Holy Spirit's point. First of all, I was not the worst in the world, no matter how I felt. Secondly, I had to stay positive in faith and give no room to the devil.

On we went into the next round of the battle. From my behaviour at home, my husband surmised that this was probably a stronger controlling spirit we were dealing with. This proved to be the extremely powerful Ruling Prince Jezebel, ruler of all deception, perversion and witchcraft. It greatly resisted the command to leave, and several times we had to stop, as I thought it was surely going to kill me before it left, such was the physical pain it caused. Again I returned home completely exhausted and remembering little of what had happened. The spiritual power of the spirit had affected even other meetings which were going on in the church building that morning. But the Lion of the Tribe of Judah had prevailed even against this powerful prince of darkness. To think that on Calvary, Jesus Christ of Nazareth took on the whole host of hell, from the greatest to the least – even Satan himself – and all on his own He overcame them, making a public spectacle of them. We need never be intimidated by what hell might array against us as the people of God; we have a mighty conquering King as our Lord.

When I recovered from this deliverance, I knew

I was a different person. The spirit of control which had been cast out of my life many months ago, certainly no longer drove me. But now I found I could completely let go in areas I had not even been aware of. I could approach situations with transparency ready to meet whatever or whoever awaited me. I discovered a new spontaneity in my reactions as situations no longer needed to be consistently weighed and measured in order for me to cope with them. In an even deeper way, I no longer needed to feel on top of everything or involved with everything. I could now relax and operate in the sphere which God had given me and not concern myself in a wrong way with things beyond me. I found I could now take a real interest in situations and people which may in the past have seemed peripheral or unimportant to me. Position no longer mattered to me at all, and I was just as content to "fade into the background" of the Fellowship, as to function in any ministry there. More than ever I was now able to acknowledge and appreciate my husband as the head of our home. This controlling spirit is so strong and dominant, that it despises those it considers weaker than itself, and will only give way to a stronger demon, and of course, to the authority of the Lord Jesus Christ. Our lives began to flow together in a new way and our marriage has continued to be greatly blessed and enriched since then.

# Chapter Twelve

With the official opening of the Apostolic New Life Centre, Bray, scheduled for June 1st 1990, we pressed on in our intercession for the completion of the work and the expansion of the kingdom of God in our midst. I continued to strengthen myself in the Lord and in relationships, now that I no longer felt threatened by people. At times I still found it difficult to enter confidently into spiritual warfare, and decided to listen to a set of teaching cassettes on the subject, to build myself up. As I listened one day to some teaching on confronting the enemy in the name of Jesus, to my surprise I found my self confronted instead. Although I did not physically see or hear anything, I recognised by the effect on my body and spirit, that an evil spirit was communicating with me with menacing threats if I should dare to defy it. My heart was pounding, and my legs seemed to have melted into the ground; I knew what it was that had spoken, but was it internal or external that was the question that worried me. Was this a "close encounter of the demonic kind"? or another manifestation of a spirit within? Whatever it was, I pleaded the blood of Jesus against it, and said "Whatever or wherever you are, I will defy you in the Name of Jesus." I would never underestimate or treat lightly the power of these demons, but after all I had been through, I was not going to be intimidated by any demon. I then put the experience aside and left it with the Lord.

Yet I could not quite regain my peace. After two months of relating so well to others, I began to feel very uncomfortable talking with Christians. I could engage in very ordinary conversation alright, but I could not bear to hear them talk about the Lord. I again found I could not listen to the Word of God being preached, in fact any situation where the life of God was being shared and ministered, made me want to run away screaming. Obviously, it was very difficult to be involved in a Fellowship feeling like this. More and more I found myself over-reacting to death wherever I witnessed it. Television news, documentaries even soppy movies, produced in me a great sense of grief and mourning and weeping. It was as if death itself were inside of me, the reality and horror of it being relived over and over again. I thought often of my brother's death and grieved and grieved for him. Around this time I read a magazine article referring to a memorial service for the victims of the Great Hunger, the Irish Famine of the 1800s. This article suggested that the fact that we Irish as a nation have experienced such suffering and deprivation in our past, would explain why we relate so closely and generously to those starving in the Third World today. Suffering, it contended, is perhaps a part of the Irish psyche, an unconcious memory which now motivates us and links us to present day suffering. I read the article in the light of what I was now experiencing. There was certainly something within me which was linking me to the death which I now saw around me. But it was more than an unconscious memory. I was beginning to understand that it was the spirit of death itself, a spirit which pervades the Irish personality with its fear and melancholy destruction.

It was time to come back and seek help again, and thus I found myself in the throes of the last battle against the ruling spirit of death and hell. It had finally left with all its horror, when Pastor spoke to me "Carmel, I think you know this last spirit, I think it has communicated with you". I was shocked. Surely he did not think I was deliberately hiding or covering up for some demon. This had not been all just a game. "I am referring to that spirit that spoke to you and threatened you", he said. The Holy Spirit had shown him that this was a personal guiding spirit, which had been sent into my life with the commission to destroy me. This was to be the last and the strongest of all, this spirit of destruction which had become so completely a part of my personality. Exactly how long it had lodged there I did not know, but it had probably acted as host to all the others. If even this last one was left undisturbed, it could have in time provided a "landing ground" for other demons to come back in. Praise the Lord for the gift of discerning of spirits to the body of Christ.

Obviously I would have to renounce this spirit. To do so should not have posed any problem to me, yet, in that twilight spiritual world, as I closed my eyes to pray, the spirit seemed to plead with me to let it stay, trying to play on my sympathy. "How can you turn me out after all I have done for you?" What a deceiver. All it had ever done was to bring ruin and waste into my life. Now it was going to leave.

If you have read the first pages of this testimony you will know that this last demon prince did indeed leave, but not without a struggle and a fight. As always, Jesus was the victor in the end, and although we were all exhausted, we knew of a surety, that had been the last battle in deliverance for me. Somewhat like a prisoner released after serving a long jail sentence, the next step would be to learn to cope with life "on the outside". It did not prove to be easy.

Although these spirits were now on the outside, they did not take lightly to being evicted from their regular stomping ground, and hounded me for the next two weeks. Instead of being full of the joy of the Lord, I was wretched and wrecked. I felt all the negative feelings I had ever felt in those weeks and just wanted to crawl into a corner and lick my wounds. If I thought I was going to get sympathy for poor old me after all I had been through, I was seriously wrong. Both the pastor and my husband saw the danger for me if I should just run away now, or lie down and die. I had to get quickly back on my feet and face life and the enemy in whatever form he presented himself, and he seemed to present himself at this time in the form of every demon that had ever influenced my life. Rejection, rebellion, anger, suicide, they all seemed to press in on me in those days. I was even afraid to withdraw from the battle against the enemy long enough to really spend time with God. I thought if I took my eyes off what was going on outside, I would just be overrun. In the end I began to suspect that perhaps I was not free after all, but nobody would believe that.

Eventually, the pressure broke, proving that the enemy could not keep up a sustained attack against the name and the blood of Jesus. The worst of the battle now seemed to be over, but yet my heart seemed so far from God. I got on my knees and cried "Lord, what is wrong with me? I should be full of love and gratitude to you, but my heart is cold". It was then I recalled Jesus' words to Peter "*When thou art converted, strengthen thy brethren*" (Luke 22.32 AV) The Holy Spirit showed me in that moment that now that I was free, now that my heart and decisions were truly my own, I again had to make a choice, whether to go on with Him or not. My heart in a sense, now free, had again to be "converted" and committed to following the Lord. But the decision was mine to make. Even though He had done so much for me, He still would not lord it over me, He was still a gentleman. It was up to me to choose life. When I understood these things, I was again able to humbly submit my heart to Him and rededicate my life to serving Him and His people. With this decision, I turned the corner, and stepped out into light and life, never I trust, to look back again. I had faced my greatest fears, confessed my deepest guilt, and could face life now as a real person with nothing to hide.

Almost a year has passed since that day. If I were asked to sum up what has been achieved in my life in that year, I would say in a word, "consistency"; that longed for quality of life that so eludes those of us who are subject to personality disorders and mood swings. I know now the sheer joy of being able to face every morning with a smile regardless of the ordinary difficulties of life and the trials of our faith.

It has been a year of learning to be part of the answer rather than part of the problem in our home and Fellowship, a year when the tears of rage and despair have been replaced by tears of compassion for others. A year of discovery of myself and my true God-given personality and abilities. A year in which I have been led down avenues once fraught with pain and failure, only to find them reclaimed by the power of God.

Apart from the occasional re-evaluation of my progress and growth in God, there has been no need for ongoing counsel and ministry, no need for any additional "props" to maintain my victory and freedom in Christ. In commitment to the regular disciplines of Christian life, to prayer, fellowship, study and faith in the Word of God, and giving and receiving within the body of Christ, I have found that Jesus Himself is the sustainer of all things, holding all things (including me) together by His powerful Word (Hebrew 1:3). Whether the future holds little or much by the world's standards, I know I have found in Him at last what no one can take away. He is my security, my joy, my hope, my self-worth. He has become my all in all.

# Conclusion

I realise that some of you reading this testimony may find it theologically difficult to accept. Yet a careful study of the Word of God reveals what a vital part of Jesus' ministry, and the ministry of the apostles, deliverance was. Jesus came to destroy all the work of the evil one, and this must surely apply in every area of the life of the believer. The Bible tells us "*The whole world is under the control of the evil one*" (1 John 5:19 NIV), and we ignore the spiritual implications of this fact at our peril.

But others of you I know will have related all too well to my life of struggle and defeat. To you I say, be reconciled to God. Jesus has paid the highest price for your life and liberty; the price was his blood shed on Calvary. You now have the right as a blood-washed child of God to live a life of peace, love and freedom. You have the legal right in God to healing and restoration emotionally, psychologically and spiritually. You have the right, but more so, the responsibility to become more like Jesus every day, serving Him as an effective member of His army in these last days. In the ministry of deliverance God has equipped His church to deal with the hidden internal enemy which is so often the cause of our defeat. How can we neglect such a great salvation?

I challenge you today to say with King David

of old "*I pursued my enemies and overtook them, I did not turn back till they were destroyed . . . I beat them as fine as dust borne on the wind*". (Psalm 18:37, 42 NIV) Freedom is yours, but the choice is also yours. Are you prepared today to take those first steps in your own individual "Fight to Freedom"?